EMS MY WAY:

A Collection of Stories & Insights
from an EMS Pioneer

LOU JORDAN

© Lou Jordan 2020

ISBN: 978-1-09830-289-4

eBook ISBN: 978-1-09830-290-0

TABLE OF CONTENTS

INTRODUCTION

Foreward:

Over the past 55 to 60 years, I have had many experiences in emergency services, and trying to put them together has been difficult because of the overlap of so much of the different activities I've been involved with. These include my youth, time in the Army, my years with the fire department, my time with the Shock Trauma Unit in Baltimore, time with the Hostage Rescue Team of the FBI, and personal experiences and growth. For a long period of time I've been wanting to put down my life experiences to share them with others. The intent of this is not to impress anyone, as I'm sure there are others that have accomplished much more over their lifetimes. My experiences have gone from one to the other, to the other, with one common thread through them, and that has been helping people through emergency medicine. It appears that there are many different aspects, and unraveling them is going to be difficult. What I want to make clear is that this is not an "I'm a Hero" book. As a publisher, I've perused many manuscripts from anyone and everyone that thinks they're a hero, and in fact, as you read most of the stories, you will see they are experiences that have been mutilated and altered from other stories that are out there. I refuse to take part in that, but I'm gonna present to you the facts as I lived and remember them.

The idea of putting down my experiences has been with me for a long time. I have always put it off despite many requests and suggestions. As I told stories to people, they would state, "You really should write this down." I delayed doing it until this stage of my life where I'm now 74 years old and medical problems make it quite clear that time is running out, and I did not want to leave this undone. I do believe I have, as many others do, unique experiences. We're gonna try and put together the pieces. Understand that there will be overlap because on some occasions I was involved in two or three different activities, such as teaching, traveling to the Caribbean and doing training, working with the Hostage Rescue Team of the FBI, working at the Shock Trauma Unit, running the first aid center at the Civic Center in Baltimore, Maryland, overseeing such great events as wrestling, roller derby, hockey games and the Ringling Brothers, Barnum & Bailey circus, and many other activities. So, this may appear to be a bit of a hodgepodge as we go along but hopefully what will happen will be, with proper editing, it'll make sense that you'll find some value in.

There are many memories that are going to be presented in this book, but one theme that should be obvious is that we were not restricted and regulated as much as those doing the job today. If we were, we wouldn't have made it long enough to get our first check! But the fact is that the old days were truly 'The Good Old Days' for me.

I feel that Fire, Police and EMS are separate and distinct professions, and that each requires individuals that are dedicated to one or the other. The initial and ongoing training required to maintain proficiency in more than one of these professions is, to say the least, difficult.

I am a firm believer in the 'Third Service Model' that each should be separate but equal, regardless of which garage you park your vehicle in.

EMS is a service that must be seen and addressed as a separate service, and not an additional duty to justify jobs and budgets of Fire Departments.

That clarified, I do believe that both Fire and EMS can complement each other…but Fire and EMS must clearly have their own command structure as they are different.

When the delivery of service is 80% EMS and 20% Fire, it is obvious that EMS needs its own identity, as it is not just something else firefighters do. It increasingly is seen as a separate and at least equal service.

Perhaps we will see some reduction in the constant Fire-vs-EMS debates, and reconciliation will take place. But I am not holding my breath.

I have many people to thank in retrospect, for there were many who for one reason or another, gave me opportunity. Some of them will be mentioned as I go further into writing this book.

Regrets? I have a number of them, but the largest is that I spent most of my life focused on work and this took its toll on my marital and family life. Often, far too often, I was asked, "What is it going to be? Me or your work?" and often I foolishly did not realize that I was a workaholic. A number of people in my life were shortchanged by my addiction to EMS.

If you learn one thing from this book, I hope it is that you look closely at family relationships, and that you give them the time and effort they need. If not, you will find that there is no going back.

Rather than attempt to write this book as a strict autobiography, I choose to present situations and occurrences as they happened, with my associated thoughts and conclusions. I do not expect that all will agree or disagree with my perspectives. I do not seek either agreement or disagreement, but to present parts of my life's experiences and hopefully provoke thought.

Having lived most of my life in the world of Emergency Services, and more specifically Emergency Medical Services, I look back with emotions of love, respect, pride, wonder and on occasion, sadness and disgust as I sort through the many memories of these past 55-60 years.

Having been blessed with many good friends, opportunities and experiences, there is a need for me to share and perhaps give back some insight.

Those of us that had, and took advantage of, the opportunity to participate in the birth and growth of EMS, are the keepers of a history of sorts. With very few exceptions, the EMS books or stories that have been written in the past have been, in my opinion, presented in a manner designed to please the reader, or glorify the writer.

I feel that the elements of truth, once glossed over or polished up to the point that they are self-serving, is worse than a lie. I believe that in order for those that will shape EMS in the future to understand the past, they should know it all, the good and the bad.

Because the majority, by far the vast majority, of those that enter the world of EMS are initially caring and impressionable individuals, they are often led astray, and may believe the stories they hear are all true. The hearts and flowers, heroic saves and warm and fuzzy feelings promised often fail to materialize. This let-down leads to a large number of individuals having their hopes and dreams destroyed. Their initial goals are often then seen as unattainable, and they find that they must either settle for less, or leave the field of EMS.

EMS is a very honorable and rewarding way to grow as a human being. It can either renew your faith in mankind, or turn you into a hardened, bitter individual.

If you can remain at your best when you are dealing with people at their worst, you have two choices. You can focus on your ability to make things better, or on others' abilities to make them worse. It is quite easy to become hard and uncaring, for you will spend many hours dealing with the results of illnesses and injuries. You will be a front-line participant in viewing and dealing with the aftermath of man's inhumanity to man, as well as seeing man's stupidity at its heights.

Those that have realistic expectations of just how much and how fast they can change things will survive and contribute. Those that do not may soon find themselves frustrated and bitter.

I often have heard people tell an EMS provider, "I couldn't do what you do." The response is usually, "Oh, you get used to it" or "It doesn't bother you after a while."

For almost 50 years I have given new students the same advice, and I still believe it applies to all EMSers: "The day you can look in the mirror and say that the pain and hurt of patients doesn't bother you, is the day you should get out of EMS. For once you don't care, once it really doesn't bother you anymore, you have lost the most valuable part of being a good EMS provider—your caring."

It is a strange quirk of our field that leads us to designate a call as a 'good one' when the intensity of death, pain and suffering is used as the measurement. Think about it...the worse it is for someone else, the greater the chance we will describe it as a 'good call.'

Your seeking the 'good calls,' and the elusive 'big one,' will make you lose focus on the importance of the everyday sick case, bump on the head, upset stomach call that you respond to. EMS isn't about heroes; it's about people helping people.

In my estimation heroes are the folks that do their best for everyone, they are those that don't know where the cameras are, and don't care. Do your best and someday, because of fate you may be called a hero. Do your best and you will always be a hero, recognized or not.

The world needs more heroes...

Dedication:

I was told that every book needs a dedication, and I find that I could write a dedication that perhaps equals the book in length. I have many people to thank for all the opportunities, support and encouragement they have given me through my life.

On the family side,

To my wife Marion, who was willing to take a chance, and showed me a new focus, on life and love for the past 22 years.

To my parents and stepparents, who have been there through good and bad times.

To my siblings who are always just a call away.

To the mother of my children, Ruth, and the ladies in my earlier life that allowed me to grow and achieve.

To my children that have made me so proud of how they live their lives. They grew up playing victims in EMS training programs, models in EMS textbooks, working as rescuers at high-speed boat races, always understanding their Daddy's EMS addiction. While other kids were going to movies or the swimming pool, mine were being extricated from junk cars and bandaged by EMT trainees. They certainly had a different childhood.

But most of all to my grandchildren, who revitalized my life with a new and wonderful love at a time when I thought that I knew all there was to know about love.

On the professional side,

To my friends and role models, Harvey Grant, Jim Gargan, Bob Murray, Jim Page, Bob Motley, Cecil Arnold, Norm McSwain, MD, Rocco Morando, David Boyd, MD and Chief Marty McMahon, some of the EMS dinosaurs that made EMS happen.

To the many co-workers that contributed to Shock Trauma growing from a 2-bed 'Death Lab' to the leading Trauma Center model that has been copied around the world.

To the many EMSers that have been a part of making this world a better place.

And most importantly, to a friend whose vision and belief established EMS as a needed and recognized medical care system, R Adams Cowley, MD. His respect and guidance of field caregivers worldwide was as important to EMS as the Star was to Bethlehem. I will never forget working for and with you. While I often called you "Boss," our friendship was never based on social status, but on respect and belief. I will always think of you as the closest of friends, and I think of and miss you often. "RA, you are missed and not forgotten."

I thank you all.

About this book:

Due to the fact that many of the individuals mentioned in this book are still living, and that the facts are written as I remember them, I have purposely taken steps to protect a number of individuals by leaving out their names. While I remember many, and will obviously miss mentioning some, a few are not mentioned by design.

All of the incidents described in this book are true and factual, and I will not bore you with all the weird stories I have heard repeated in so many other EMS books, as most of them, I believe, are always a friend of a friend of somebody that knew somebody, etc. etc. These include drying a kitten in the microwave, and the individual sitting on a toilet, lighting a cigarette in a fog of hairspray and burning his backside, and the attendants laughing so hard they dropped him off the stretcher and broke his arm. These and many other stories have popped up over the years, and I'm sure as you continue your career, you'll bump into some of these legends that people have a desire to be their stories. There are many stories that all of us could tell, but these are the ones that stick out in my mind as I look back.

There are those among us that have used EMS, and the people in it, for their own self-serving interests. It really doesn't matter who they are, their names need not be known. But I am sure many of you will be able to identify someone just like them; there are still some in the EMS world. Do your best to expose them or find a way to avoid them…just don't consider being one. They don't belong.

I will let the readers make their own judgements.

lcj

YOUTH

I was born on January 1, 1943 (yes, a New Year's Baby) in Quincy, Massachusetts, a small city just south of Boston. My youthful and teenage years were unremarkable. The oldest of three boys in a middle-class family, I was by most standards your neighborhood kid that along with his friends made the same mistakes that kids have since time began. I can easily relate my life to the era of Happy Days, the TV program that depicted the 50s and 60s. Our hangout was Jack's Dairy Bar, located across the street from the High School.

Smoking at 13, drinking not much after that, and playing that 'Gawdawful' Rock and Roll music too loud was typical of kids in those days. Fortunately, we were not a part of the drug culture that came along later. We were high on life and friends, and for the most part we were looking forward to the end of school and getting a good job. My goal was to have a job that paid me lots of money and required little to no work. That future became a cloud of dust when reality struck. My climb to success had elevated me to a 16-year-old supervisor of 2 part-time 15-year-old kids that sorted returned soda bottles in a large supermarket.

Growing older and wiser through the years, I had many opportunities that fortunately helped me grow as an individual and reach various levels of success.

I grew up, or perhaps it would be more appropriate to say, spent my early years, in a small town in New England. I am not sure if I have finished growing up yet. Past 70 I still learn things, and rethink some of the things I have known for a long time. On occasion I reaffirm an old belief or adjust it due to new circumstances or information.

I went to high school in Braintree, Massachusetts, south of Boston. Its greatest distinction at that time was that it was where most traffic from the North turned to get to Cape Cod. Since that time, it has become a victim of urban sprawl, growth, expansion or whatever we now call responsible for turning small, warm towns where everyone was friendly, left their doors unlocked and talked with their neighbors, into crowded and impersonal communities.

One often hears children express their desire to be a fireman, policeman and more recently a paramedic when they grow up. Not me. I never had a dream of being a policeman, a fireman or an ambulance driver, as they were known in those days.

Things were different then; there were different values. As kids we had our growing pains getting into mischief and having the local police either swat us on the back of the head, or even worse, bring us home to our parents. We knew and respected the police in our town, but we still stretched our antics to the limit.

The Fire Department was never a place to hang around in our town. The doors were usually closed and the firefighters were not involved with the community very much. They were probably resting up for their "other" job, which they all had. Some things never change.

Most of the time I was around the firefighters in my youth was when we visited the police station, as both departments shared a common building. Perhaps part of the reason we didn't see the firemen was that we were usually in a hurry to profess our innocence and get out of the police station.

My earliest memory of firefighters is focused on the swearing individuals that had to shovel snow away from the hydrants during the cold winters. They were also the same group of guys that would come with lights and sirens waking up everyone along their route of travel.

I, like many civilians of today, had no idea why they had to break every window in a house and chop holes in the roof when the fire was obviously in only one room. I found out later, when I became a firefighter.

It wasn't hard to get a little excitement in our sleepy town; you just had to pull down the hook in the red box on the corner. Within a short period of time, the firefighters would be there with their usual grumbles and swearing, which delighted us youthful passersby who 'just happened' to be in the area.

At that time, the Town of Braintree Police Department ran the ambulance service. I guess they chose the Police Department because the police were always on the street, perhaps they didn't have other jobs, or perhaps it was because they weren't always swearing at everyone.

I had the opportunity to ride in the hearse-type ambulance only one time, as a 16-year-old teenager. A number of us had attended the annual company picnic put on by the owners of the local supermarket. I became violently ill as I was driving home, with vomiting, uncontrollable diarrhea and profuse sweating. When I arrived, I fell to the front lawn and called for help. After swearing on a proverbial stack of bibles that I hadn't been drinking, I was carried into the house and an ambulance was called. I have often wondered if I would have been left on the lawn if I HAD been drunk.

When the driver of the ambulance approached the front of the house, I recognized his gruff voice asking, "who is it?" It was Officer Buddy Davenport, probably the biggest guy on the force. My mother said it was her son, and he immediately called to me by name assuring me that he would be right there.

He was both a hulk of a man and a gentle giant at the same time. He gently picked me up and carried me in his arms to the ambulance. On the way to the hospital, he told us that 13 people from the party were being treated for food poisoning. A well-intentioned, but relatively stupid, host had sprayed for flies in the tent housing the food. Additionally, the grill had been painted silver prior to cooking the hot dogs and hamburgers. We all recovered and had great stories to tell about the 'garden hose' lavage we had experienced.

That was my only exposure to an ambulance during my youth. Come to think of it, that was enough.

Quite frankly, until my early 20s, all I wanted was to get an easy job making big money. In retrospect I guess you could say I was part of a generation that was 'looking for myself,' but I didn't realize I was lost.

ARMY

Through some stroke of luck my senior year grades were adequate for me to get an early graduation from high school to enter military service. So, in January of 1960, six of my friends and I were given our diplomas and shipped out to the Army's basic training center at Ft. Dix, NJ.

We ended up scattered around the world and most of us lost touch. It was a rude awakening to go from carefree kid to a recruit that was held responsible for their actions. It was also a culture shock to find that 'All men are created equal' was not practiced in the Army.

All recruits were no longer individuals with decision-making abilities; we were like a set of legs on a centipede. If you got out of step the guy in front or back stepped on you, and if the centipede had one screw up, the entire unit paid the price and suffered the consequences. It was amazing how the peer pressure brought our individualists into team thinking. And it was not just marching that required team effort, it was virtually everything. You were judged on your individual effort to the team.

That time in my life made me realize that it doesn't have to be about you, but about what the collective "You's" on the team do together to attain a desired result. Team wins made it a benefit for all the team players. That lesson has helped me greatly through the years. Even when in a command situation, a supervisor or instructor or business owner, I knew that being the boss doesn't make you have all the answers. Having the staff or class involved and aware of the goals often motivates them greatly. If they know the task and have ideas how to attain those goals, a smart leader will listen and consider implementing the ideas that are feasible to get the desired result. It is not the tail wagging the dog; it is the dog knowing how to get the tail wagging.

Joining the US Army immediately after High School was for me, and most other GI's, the first real exposure to discipline. While I certainly didn't like the way the Army ran things, I soon found that they were less than receptive to suggestions from a 17-year-old recruit. I decided to play their game.

The military was an experience that certainly helped me develop some of the work ethics and responsibility that have helped me in life. I quickly realized that being a team player was not an act of giving up your independence. It is controlling your independence.

I learned that building a greater sense of belonging and sharing in the pride that came from team success is quite rewarding. While there is a time to lead, quite often clear direction and an understanding of the goal will allow the group dynamics to accomplish the task with much less effort. I have found that most leaders that I respected in life have been those that were a functional part of the team.

My army experiences were of extreme value although I didn't realize it at the time. They gave me the opportunity to see that being part of a team wasn't so difficult, and that the team could accomplish more than the individual could. I also had the opportunity to meet many people from many different walks of life, with different backgrounds educationally, religiously, and racially, and in the service, we were required to work as a team and to put aside the problems or concerns we had with people that were different than us. I found quickly that the military does meld people together and I found it to be one of the most rewarding building blocks of my life. I still maintain contact with some of my counterparts after all this time.

I started as an MP at Fort Gordon, GA. From there, I was sent to a secret atomic energy site in Texas, then went to Fort Meade, MD in 1962, where I was trained as a field medic. That was my first exposure to EMS-type work. I served with the 36th Evacuation Hospital, which was a field hospital similar to the medical mobile army surgical hospital organization that gained fame in the television series M*A*S*H*. Our rudimentary caregiving was splinting, bleeding control, and hopefully the restoration of breathing. A MASH unit consists of a convoy of trucks and people that carry and build a complete circus of tents that are magically transformed into a complete hospital. From the admissions area to the morgue, from the kitchen to the laundry, from the labs to the motor pool, it is an inter-dependent marvel.

Stationed there, I had other lessons in just how important teamwork was. From putting up the tents, to setting up the hospital laundry, every part of the team depended on the other. If one section failed, we all suffered.

In spite of the pride of being associated with the 36th, I knew for sure that the Army was not where I would spend my life. In spite of my attempts to improve the Army, they repeatedly refused to accept my constructive criticism.

"Why?" I asked, must we be awakened at 5 AM when we cannot eat breakfast until 7:30? "Why?" must we be rushed out of a warm bed to stand in line in the dark and the cold at 5:15 to be counted? We were all neatly lying in beds in straight rows, and could have been counted by the poor fool assigned to walk among us all night lest we be attacked in our sleep. "Why?" must we schedule our vacations 12 months ahead of time, when we can't possibly know when and where next week's parties will be held? These and many other mysteries were not answered to my satisfaction during my 3 years of service. I determined that it was time for me to enter the civilian world and get started on finding my easy job with the big salary.

Six months prior to my discharge, I had found Ms. Perfect, the first one, and got married. With a wife and a baby on the way, it was obvious that GI pay was not going to lead me to wealth, and the prospect of being transferred to some outpost without my family was even less appealing. I took my honorable discharge in February 1963 and entered the civilian world in nearby Baltimore, Maryland.

I found work in many different fields those first few months. From painter, to landscaper, driver and warehouse worker, I brought home the bacon, while becoming more and more disillusioned with my progress on the ladder of success. Answering an ad for a job at the local Revere Copper and Brass Foundry was the answer to our prayers. I ran an annealing furnace, the hourly wage was good, time and ½ was plentiful, and with the bonus incentives our income was 8 times what the Army had provided. We were able to purchase our first home before I was even 21.

While we were doing well financially, I was working 12 hours a day, 6 or 7 days a week. I realized that I had only accomplished half of my goal. I was making lots of money, but I had not found the easy way to do it.

The neighbor across the street was my age, and would oftentimes be seen sitting on his front steps just relaxing while the rest of us were going to work or coming home. He seemed to always be relaxing, taking vacations and driving new cars.

I found that he was a firefighter with the Baltimore City Fire Department. His work schedule allowed him to get in his duty hours and have plenty of time off. When he was on night shift, 5 PM to 7 AM, he was more often than not able to sleep all night. I compared his '4 shifts and 72 hours on; 4 shifts and 48 hours off' schedule with my demanding 72 to 84 hours a week. With his scheduled vacation days, etc., he had 9 vacations a year, of 9 days each. Now this was just the kind of job I was looking for!

I took the next civil service exam and was hired. Even though I took a 50% reduction in salary, I found that I had time for my family and a life of my own.

My happiness with the decision to compromise on the money in order to have a reasonable life was short-lived. I found that as a firefighter, I filled much of my off-duty time with side jobs to bring in extra income. This is a very common practice for civil service employees, especially those on the lower end of the pay scale. I attribute the need to hold down two jobs as one of the contributing factors to the high divorce rates found with Police, Fire and EMS workers.

FIREFIGHTING

Entering the Baltimore City Fire Department (BCFD) and Fire School was not a very eventful or remarkable part of my life. I was, after all, looking for a paycheck and a job where I could sleep and get paid. However, the team spirit and similarity to the military teamwork of the Army quickly brought back the spirit that I had experienced in the Army. Being a part of a team had its advantages. While you had responsibilities, you had team mates that helped guide you along and showed you the ropes. I was surprised that as much as I had wanted out of the military, the Fire Department's para-military structure was quite comfortable. The crew and officers wanted to make me a part of the team, as they knew that their lives might be influenced by my actions. The brotherhood was evident from the beginning. I also knew that my life might depend on them, and I wanted to be sure that if the proverbial feces hit the fan, that they would be there for me as well.

My time with the fire department was very enlightening, probably as much if not more so than the period of time I spent in the army. While I do not condone any of the activities that the department was engaged in and the individuals were engaged in, you need to realize that this was a different time in our country's history. Baltimore is a city that is mostly black; however, the fire department was traditionally white and was going through the growth factor of bringing a more representative group of individuals into the department. This was not an easy task and quite frankly it met with much opposition, as most firefighters were fathers and sons, brothers, uncles and family members. Pretty much if you had a family member or a strong friend in the department, somehow your name could appear on the list and you could have a job there.

On the other side of this coin was the drive to integrate the department. This led to a lot of contention and what later was to be looked upon as unfair adjustments being made, as it totally affected those firefighters that were already in the ranks, as they saw the new people coming in being given a special advantage. The affirmative action programs, in their attempts to catch up, I believe went overboard in that they were out very aggressively recruiting anyone and everyone to join the department if they were of the black race. Special programs were set up to train individuals from inner-city areas, mostly black, and they were tutored to pass the exams. This created quite an animosity in the fire department, as it has in other departments, as our society changed to be more inclusive.

However, when we were off the fire grounds, when we returned to quarters or other duties, we went back into our own separate worlds. At that time, the toilet facilities where I was stationed had separate toilets that were black, and actually had black seats. Those of us that were white showered separately, we cooked food separately and ate separately, and the separation was quite obvious.

After a period of time it became pretty obvious to those of us that were on the job, that when we went on a call, we had to depend on one another to have our backs, get the job done, and get it done safely. Over the years, comradeship built.

My years with the BCFD during the 60's and 70's saw much change and were important building blocks in my life. My firefighting duties and experiences took place at a time very different than today. I started out as a back-step firefighter that used to hang on to the back or sides of a piece of fire apparatus when responding to calls. Those days are long gone, as firefighters now are kept inside the apparatus and seat belted when responding. Nothing will ever replace the thrill of hanging on a bouncing piece of apparatus as it sped down the street. Regardless of the weather, we were seen clutching the rail or the ladder. Often, we were finishing putting on our boots and rubber raincoats while holding on with one hand. The public stopped to see us pass by, often waving at us, as if we were in a parade. However, statistics caught up with us nationally, and the number of injuries and deaths resulted in the implementation of safer ways of getting from the station to the scene. BCFD lost a member of my class of rookies shortly after going to our duty stations. Falling off the apparatus was now seen up close and personal as a dangerous practice by everyone. It was a great thrill, but it needed to be recognized for its danger, and addressed, and is now a tradition of the past. Today we sit inside on contoured seats with seatbelts and headsets. Heat and air-conditioned comfort sure beat the rain and snow of riding outside.

While we did have radio communications, we still utilized the old fire alarm 'Street, Box' system of numbered bells that corresponded with numbered fire alarm boxes located throughout the city. The equipment at the desk made hash marks on a strip of paper noting where the call was. We got good at waking up, and getting dressed while listening to the bells. We started when the Street was coming across, and if we were half-dressed when the Box came across, and we recognized it as not one of ours, we could go back to sleep.

Radios were being utilized as a backup or redundant system to give us further information, while responding and on location. Later on, we had hand-held radios for the officers.

Today's firefighters have standard protocols and advanced equipment that is mandated to be utilized, such as breathing apparatus, turn-out gear and flame-resistant uniforms. In my day, we wore regular khaki work clothes and with the addition of a raincoat and boots and a helmet, we fought fires. Shortly the cumbersome turn-out gear began to be issued and we were much better protected.

The apparatus had one self-contained breathing apparatus (SCBA) on board. This was the compressed air cylinder and mask that is commonly in use today. However, the air pack and mask were seldom utilized, as real firefighters weren't afraid of a little smoke. It was generally considered that those utilizing the mask really were not real firefighters as they weren't eating the smoke as tradition dictated. Masks were for 'sissies.' Many of the 'Smoke Eaters' of my day were later found to have various forms of lung disease. We just didn't know the price of being a 'Smoke Eater.'

We were also equipped with much lighter-weight MSA filter masks, which consisted of the facemask and hose that led to a filter canister that strapped on your chest. Breathing through these masks was not unlike trying to draw air through a mattress. Most often they were utilized sparingly and only in the worst of conditions. These masks not only hindered breathing, but also made it virtually impossible to verbally communicate with other firefighters. We hated them.

Also available were cumbersome CHEMOX breathing devices. I think they were surplus from the Navy which used them for escape from submerged submarines or ships. This was a cumbersome and complicated device that consisted of a pair of rubber lungs attached to a face piece and it contained a chemical container that generated oxygen into the lungs of the device. It worked based on the chemicals in the container being activated by your expired breath and the moisture in your exhalation. To utilize this device, you would blow air into the mask inflating the lungs with your expired air. The chemical reaction added oxygen into your expired air, which you then re-breathed. It had a tendency to overinflate the rubber lungs and build over-pressure in the lungs which then had to be manually vented. In addition to the bulkiness and weight of such a unit, the more you exerted yourself, the more often you had to release pressure. These devices were never really used except in training drills.

I believe that the complexity and newness of the concept of respiratory protection for firefighters, was diametrically opposed to the macho bravado of 'real' smoke eaters. We fought fires and experienced the choking smoke and its resultant discharge of foul colored sputum and nasal drainage. Those were the badges and indicators we used to identify real firefighters in days gone by.

I recall in retrospect the many times we would be coughing and spitting from a 'belly full' of smoke and would sit on the tailboard of the engine, in a cloud of exhaust from the tailpipe, smoking a cigarette, gagging and wiping nasal drainage off our faces. That was our rehab!!!

Like all rookies I learned from the experienced firefighters with whom I worked and lived. My first station house, Engine 50, was a low call volume station located in the heavily industrial area near Baltimore's Inner Harbor and Marine terminal. The station was surrounded by railroad tracks that were quite active. One set of tracks blocked two of the three ways we could go when leaving quarters. Frequently when we got a call, we found that a train of autos from the GM plant would be wrapped around our station and we would have to sit there while the incredibly slow train moved forward and back, dropping cars on the side tracks. I learned to hate trains.

We got a call once to the General Motors plant for a bomb scare, and everybody did a walk-through looking for a bomb. While we had many bomb scares, most of us realized our odds of finding a bomb in an auto assembly plant was an exercise in futility.

Another bomb scare call at the Pittsburgh Paint & Glass factory gave us some real excitement, though. On completion of our bomb search, we were sitting on one of the docks eating lunch. The sun was going down, and the heat on some nearby oil drums caused them to expand with loud bangs. I've never seen so many firefighters run so fast in my life.

At the American Standard smelting company, another firefighter and I were walking down a hallway, and the captain was walking between the two of us. We didn't see any smoke or anything, then all of a sudden, the captain grabs the back of our jackets and pushes us down. All three of us went to the floor and fire came out over us, and it was just like flashover in the movies. The captain had felt the pressure change coming down the hall. That was another time that someone else's experience saved us. And I learned how quickly fire could travel.

Seeking more action, I transferred to a station in a more commercial neighborhood, Engine 41, which also housed Truck 20, Chemical One, and the Deputy Chief responsible for half the city. This gave me the opportunity to work on various pieces of apparatus and expand my experiences and capabilities. It was there that I trained for the ambulance service.

One fire call from Engine 41 that stands out, we pulled up to a rowhouse, the place is fully charged with smoke. We got up and I had the axe and I broke the window. We were up on the first roof of the summer kitchen and I broke the window and I started to put my leg in to get in, and all of a sudden, I get grabbed by the back of my jacket and pulled back out. Another firefighter took the axe and held it through the window facing down to check the floor. Well, it had been a rowhouse they turned into a bank, and the smoke was really thick and you couldn't see anything. With every other rowhouse I'd been in, you'd go through that window and you're on the second floor, usually in the summer kitchen. But with this one, they had a split stairwell in there, going all the way down. If it hadn't been for him teaching me to always check to make sure there's a floor, I would have fallen about 25 feet into the basement. And it turns out that the place wasn't even on fire – they were fumigating and that's why the whole building was fully charged with smoke coming out the doors. Nobody had notified the fire department.

We also had a little girl, probably about seven years old, on O'Donnell Street. It was the middle of the night, it was dark and we went into the house, and the stairs and everywhere was all packed with newspapers and other stuff all over the place. The neighbors were screaming, "There's a kid in there!" We got in there, and tried to go up the stairs but couldn't get far, and then the guys broke the second story front window with the ladder and they came in the window. We found out later that the girl was lying right underneath the window and they might have even stepped on her, but she wasn't alive. When we got back outside, the mother is coming back from the bar and she's screaming, "My baby! My baby!" and a couple of the guys went off on her for leaving her daughter alone. Then a guy came around the corner, who was the father, and he started beating on her. The cops locked both of them up, but that was really sad, losing that little girl.

In addition to numerous dwelling fires, the majority being rowhouses which linked together a whole row of houses with a common roof, we were also called to many warehouse fires, which being larger buildings, had greater potential for intense fire.

One, I remember that when I got there, they were already running the hoses from the fire boat, which uses a lot of water. As we went up the ladders, they were putting so much water out that we could see the water coming through the bricks. We got off the ladders pretty quickly, and not much later the wall came down.

There was also a fire at a licorice storage warehouse that was not too far from our house. There were large, smoldering bales of licorice, and we spent 4 days eating, sleeping and bailing water while the thick smoke blanketed the neighborhood. The licorice had a sweet smell and taste, and nobody realized it was a laxative until the guys had eaten it for awhile.

Baltimore's Inner Harbor was predominantly warehouses, and we went through a period of time where we routinely had fires in that area. The city had a plan to develop the Inner Harbor, and miraculously we had warehouse fires very frequently. In most instances we just let them burn and waited for the bulldozers and cranes to show up on the scene and demolish what was left. Many of us felt we were being part of the revitalization of the Inner Harbor as debris was being taken out of the area.

Whole blocks of city rowhouses suffered a similar fate with almost routine timing. One or two vacant houses in a block mysteriously broke into fire as well. This cleared out residential neighborhoods.

One night we are at 41 Engine and the alarm goes off. We hear the street address and the guy on the watch desk yells out, "That's Stinky's house!" Stinky was one of our firefighters, a tillerman. It wasn't far from the station, and Stinky jumped off the back of the truck to run to the house, and another guy jumped right into the tillerman seat, just slid right in and took over. You could almost feel Stinky's heart beating as he ran to the house to get his family out.

During Fire Prevention Week, all the stations competed to have the best display. One year when I was at Station 41, the guys used an old washing machine motor and other parts, and some carpeting, and made a Sparky the Dog. We got prizes donated and had a drawing contest for the kids. We got so many prizes we used the storefront next door to hold them all. Nuns from the local school picked the winning drawings.

As a firefighter, I took a number of different training courses, like the Baltimore City Civil Defense Training Program, where I was certified as a Radiological Meter Operator. One of the classes I took was specifically geared toward ambulance service, which led me to another role at the fire department.

MEDIC DUTY

The BCFD operated a number of emergency ambulances at that time. Working on the ambulances only required that one have American Red Cross first aid training. Due to my prior experience as an Army medic, I spent a day and a half attending the course, to refresh my skills and meet the requirement of having a current card. Returning to work, I was assigned to the station that housed Engine 23, a Deputy Chief, and Ambo 1, which was located in the heart of downtown Baltimore. It's since been moved to the now famous Super D.

After my time with Ambo 1, I moved to Ambo 10. [Years later when my son applied to the department (without my knowledge), he was accepted and assigned to Ambo 10 as well. He was even given the same shift and the same Kelly number that I'd had there.]

So on my first day on the ambulance, Ambo 1, the house captain introduced me to the firefighters and the other staff, pointed out the ambulance and said, "There it is. You're in charge." I then found out that my assigned partner had recently fallen down the pole and shattered his ankle, and would be off for 8 weeks. So, I was assigned a junior firefighter to drive the ambulance, as I had no idea where the streets or the hospitals were. It was terrifying to realize that, not only did I not have an experienced partner, but that I had extremely limited knowledge of our response area or hospital locations, and that I would be working with an individual that had no desire for ambulance duty. What a great way to start!!!

While there are certainly competent firefighters that may provide ambulance service, for the most part it was clear that 'Detailed' or 'Fill in Medics' did not request ambulance duty, but were assigned in many instances as punishment duty. 'Meat Wagon,' 'Blood Bucket' and other terms of endearment for the ambulance were the norm.

The ambulance was a Schwab box ambulance, which was something relatively new at the time that I hadn't been introduced to. We quickly learned to use the street map book which listed the streets by name and the cross streets. They were actual maps with lines on them and showed which 100 block crossed over which 100 block of the cross street. Fortunately, I was in the downtown area where most of the streets ran north and south, or east and west, and due to the repetition of calls in certain areas, it didn't take long before you were familiar with where you were going, where you were heading and so on. To this day I remember the city like the back of my hand, and I can still recall the names of the streets. Because the street layouts were basically in squares with some roads going north south, and the others east-west, it trained us to drive in a quite erratic manner. As you went down the street, you would swerve from one side to the other, to be as far away from the opposing traffic should a car stick its nose into the intersection. This made for some horrendous rides. The sirens were generally mounted to the roof of the cab, and they were your federal-type sirens that just wound up and spun and spun, causing the roof of the ambulance to vibrate. It's no wonder we're all half-deaf now after so many years of driving the ambulance like that.

In the back of the ambulance were triangular bandages, gauze pads, roller bandages for bleeding control, wooden boards, and a stretcher that felt like it was made out of iron it was so heavy. We had just basic, rudimentary stuff, and then they added a suction device and oxygen on board as well for us to use as necessary, with a selection of oropharyngeal airways and an oxygen delivery system that provided liter flow oxygen.

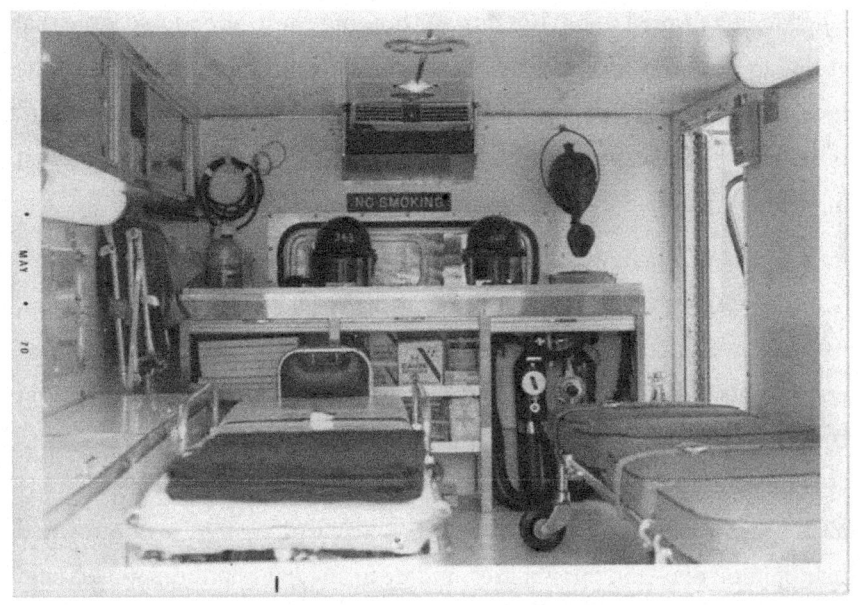

My first night and my first call on Ambo 1 was one that was memorable. We went to a rowhouse where an extremely large lady had gone to the second-and-a-half floor of her rowhouse. This was originally a two-story house and they had put a set of stairs in up to the attic, and in this little A-frame the attic wasn't very big. This large lady was in bed. The stairway was very narrow and had a 90-degree bend to it. There were two small cathedral-type windows in the front of the house. This woman was too large for us to lift on our own, so I called for the snorkel unit, which was an aerial lift firefighting device. They pulled up in the street, and raised the Stokes basket to the window, but it wouldn't fit through. We ended up pulling the mattress off the bed with the woman on it, and bumping her down the stairs on the mattress until we got to the ground floor. We backed the ambulance up on the sidewalk and brought her down the steps, and then police officers assisted us in dragging her into the back of the ambulance. When we got to University Hospital, the woman had already stopped breathing, and there was virtually nothing we could do to help her. The police had the hospital staff come outside the emergency room, and the doctor quickly pronounced the woman. We put her on a gurney and brought her to the hospital morgue, put her on a metal pallet and attempted to put her into the holding chest. She was so large that we had to push down on her belly and legs in order to get her through the door. (We often later wondered how they got her out.) When we got back to the station, the captain greeted me with, "Congratulations Jordan, you killed your first one!"

There were, I believe, 13 hospitals within the confines of Baltimore city's 50 or 55 square miles, so we were never really far from a facility. In most instances, we would go to the hospital that was on our way back to our quarters. Patients did not have the opportunity to choose which hospital they went to, as they have been in some other areas. We made the determination as to what facilities they went to. Learning the hospitals and the staff at the hospitals took a little bit of time, but it did not take very long before they formed their opinion of us and our abilities, and we formed our opinions as well, and close working relationships were developed very quickly. There were hospitals that we preferred to go to because we were welcomed and were treated as professionals. And there were hospitals that we just used to get rid of the patient after taking care of them. So there were numerous occasions where we would pick up a patient, treat them and just dump them at the hospital.

By far our favorite hospital was University Hospital, which is a long-standing facility that is also a state teaching facility. They had a great nursing staff, and had developed a great working relationship with the ambulance people. It was a catchall for most of the inner-city. It and Johns Hopkins were the two major hospitals in the city's catchment area. Not that there weren't other good hospitals, but these were large, well-established facilities and the others were smaller and still growing. It amazes me to see how they've grown over the years, from 2-story buildings to 12-story buildings. There were two or three hospitals that were run by religious groups, and the religious hospitals usually were run by Mother Superior or a nun of one denomination or another. These were very caring facilities, but they usually had limited resources. There were only a couple of hospitals that were located in extremely bad areas and were known for being extremely dangerous to be in and around.

There were a few local food places that took care of us. If it was near meal-time, we'd call a sub shop or pizza shop near the hospital, place an order and tell them about how long we'd be. We'd pick it up on our way back from the hospital, or if we were going out on a call, they'd hold it for us. We'd drive up out front and give a tap of the siren, and the girls would run outside and give us our food. They'd even share with the station house any 'extra' food that had been prepared and left over at the end of the night. But when McDonald's moved in, they put a stop to that.

One amusing story that I recall was when one of the hospitals in the inner city built their new hospital in the outskirts of the city. We spent Saturday and Sunday volunteering to transfer the patients out to the new facility. Then one night we got a call for a cutting. We responded and the address was the hospital that had just closed down. As we pulled up, we saw two security guards inside the door protecting the equipment. Leaning against the door on the outside is a guy screaming and banging on the door, with his belly cut open, and he's yelling, "Let me in!" The two security guys just have their hands on the door; they couldn't do anything anyway. But the guy's screaming and hollering, and as we start treating him, we told him it wasn't a hospital anymore. His remark was that it had been an 'F-ing' hospital since he could remember - he gets cut and suddenly it's not a hospital anymore? Like he took it personal.

On other occasions with difficult patients, those with intoxication or drugs, we often had methods that would probably cost us our jobs now. Such as taking intoxicated patients in. When the doctors said they were busy, we would often put the intoxicated patient into a high-backed wooden wheel-chair, push them down the hall towards the morgue at the end of the hall, and put a crutch through the two back wheels. We'd tie them into the chair so that they wouldn't fall out or get hurt, and they'd sit there for hours either carrying on screaming, or sleeping it off, until a doctor or staff decided they were well enough to go to jail, or to rehab or back to their halfway house.

Another fun incident that occurred on occasion was when we would get hospital staff that were not attuned to ambulance operations, and had their own way of doing things rather than a team effort, such as the ex-military nurse who was hired to take over the emergency room from 3 to 11 at the hospital in close proximity to the Greyhound bus terminal. We routinely had police and ambulances go there for man- or woman-down calls. We checked out these patients, and found out most times they were just vagrants or homeless people sleeping. The head of nursing had been very uncooperative with both the ambulance staff and police, telling us to get out of there; she didn't want us around the ER. So, what we ended up doing was in cooperation with the police. On occasion we would find the time to have two or three police officers meet us at the bus terminal. We would go through, giving the less fortunate the opportunity to go to the hospital or go to jail. It was not uncommon for us to go in with 3 or 4 patients in one ambulance, with the police following us. We would march them in and sit them down in the waiting room, fill out the paperwork as all John Does and Jane Does, and leave. It was our present to her. She was known as the 'Wicked Witch of the West.'

A life in EMS will certainly introduce you to numerous individuals that will stick in your memory. Most of these end up being either extreme calls, funny calls or the dreaded frequent flier. Frequent fliers are those that habitually utilize the EMS services with repeated calls over time. One of our all-time record holders was Ernestine, a lady in her early 30s that had no family and apparently few friends to share her life with. She lived in a one-bedroom unit with a hot plate and a picture on velvet of John Kennedy, Martin Luther King and Bobby Kennedy. She also had a princess telephone which had a light, and that was often the only light on in her room. She lived in a room on the second floor of what we would probably call a flop house, where you could have one room just for sleeping. The inside of the entire building (the stairs, the walls, even the ceiling) was all painted with silver aluminum paint, undoubtedly something that had been picked up at one of the local scrap yards and used to cover virtually all surfaces. Ernestine would call day or night, saying she needed to go to the hospital, which was only six blocks away. When we arrived, she would usually be sitting on the front steps with her nylon stockings rolled up to just below her kneecaps, a raggedy old dress, and a scarf or rag wrapped around her head. Ernestine had what she believed to be asthma, and would call us when she felt lonely. At least that's how we look at it now. Many of your frequent fliers get to be such a drain on you, sometimes going back numerous times per shift. For the most part, we would pull up and she would stand up and walk to the curb, awaiting her chauffeur to open the ambulance door. She would climb in herself, sit on the litter and start chatting with us. Ernestine was never a lights-and-siren type call. We viewed it as a social call. When we got to the hospital, we would help her out of the back of the ambulance, put her in a wheelchair and bring her into the emergency room triage area. We never found the electric eye, but there must've been one, because as we approached the triage section, Ernestine would immediately begin to gasp for breath. She did fine for the whole ride over. She referred to us as 'her boys' and thanked us for bringing her in. The staff would bring her in the back and pay her a little bit of attention, and shortly thereafter she was ready to go home. Beside the ambulance and the hospital, Ernestine had virtually no family or friends to spend time with her or help her with anything. Her life was the ambulance, the hospital and her room with the hotplate. We never saw Ernestine out on the streets walking around, although we did occasionally bump into her at the hospital while there on other calls. She quickly went from being a pain in the butt, to one of our own special characters. More than once I can recall pulling up to the front of Ernestine's place with no lights and sirens at 3 AM or so in the morning, and looking up. Ernestine would open her window and holler, "I'll be right down," and she even walked herself downstairs to the sidewalk for us to open up the door and take her to the hospital. The hospital personnel as well kind of adopted her, and responded to "Here comes Ernestine" with "Hi darling, how are you doing?" Very seldom was there any nastiness or smart remarks like, "Why don't you leave us alone," or "What are you doing here again?" We all took her under our wings and she was one of our special people.

Another special patient we had, had been born with no legs. His mode of transportation was not a wheelchair, but instead a small wooden platform with wheels on it. He used wooden blocks to propel himself along the sidewalk, or quite often the street. With his super skateboard, it was not difficult for him to relocate throughout the Monument Street neighborhood, and he irritated and agitated drivers and people on the sidewalk as he came zipping by. The problem he had was alcohol, and it amazed us that we never picked him up after being hit by a car or falling off his skateboard. However, we could not just leave him in the street, and for the police to pick him up and keep him overnight was just too much of a burden. His foaming mouth, open spitting and generally antisocial behavior made it difficult for the police to try to restrain him and keep him away from starting altercations with other prisoners. So we would grab him by the arms, put him in the ambulance and let him sleep it off at the hospital, using the emergency room as a holding tank of sorts. The easiest way for us to restrain him and keep him away from the nurses was to put him in a large, wooden wheelchair with a belt around his middle, take his hands and lash them onto the arms of the chair, and then take a crutch and put it through the wheels to prevent him from rocking back-and-forth. If he was too loud, he would generally be left in the hallway outside of the morgue where there was no one to disturb.

I remember going out one night on a call for a shooting, and we pulled up on a scene where two officers had been ambushed by members of the Black Panther Party. One officer was deceased, and the other officer had been shot seven times. Miraculously, he survived. He went to work in the Medical Examiner's Office, and we became good friends. Eventually, they did capture and jail the Black Panther members.

One day we got a call to a downtown bar in the mid-afternoon, and as we pulled up police cars were coming in, and there was a plainclothes officer down in the doorway, shot right through his badge holder. Another plainclothes officer was screaming, "Help him, Lou, he's one of ours!" We scooped him up and went to University Hospital and while we were there, we found out what had happened. A day earlier, a prisoner had been at City Hospital, and his wife walked in and gave him a gun and he escaped from the guard. That escapee had been in the bar and picked up that the plainclothes officer was a cop, so he drew a pistol and shot him. Afterward, he ran out of the bar and, after a police chase, he was cornered in a parking lot across the street. I still don't know if he shot himself or the cops shot him, but he took a bullet in the eye. So while we're down there with the officers, they bring his body in and his wife is there and she's screaming, "Why did you do this to him?" It was explained to her that SHE did this to him, and she was taken away and charged.

I very rarely told my kids about my patients, but I did sometimes to teach them safety and sometimes life lessons. Like the little boy who stuck a fork in an electric socket in the wall that they prayed for.

Another call I probably shared with my kids was the call we had for an injured person at a railroad station. We had to climb down a long hill to get to the patient. He was a boy in his late teens, who had been running on top of the cars of a moving train, and had hit the high-tension wire. His clothes had burst into flames and he fell to the side of the train, moaning and groaning. It was hard to distinguish him from the black cinders he had rolled in. We took him to the hospital, amazed he was still alive.

One little girl had stepped out of her bathtub and onto a pile of broken bottles on the floor. She was cut up real bad. A couple days later I was down-town for some reason. My son was with me, he was young and we stopped by just to see how the kid was doing. We went up the stairs and went into this stinking, hot apartment, and she's laying on the couch, with a blood-soaked bandage, all covered with flies, sweating. He got to see some less fortunate people.

One Christmas Eve we received a call for a house fire. When we arrived on location the house was pretty well involved. There were two young children who had been pulled out of the fire, a girl and a boy. The little boy was in bad shape. Another ambo had him, and we took the little girl into our ambo. She had been sleeping and had a little, white nightgown on, and it reminded me of an angel's dress. Then a full-grown male individual came in the back doors, bringing up all kinds of sputum, and we were told that he had asthma and that he had been the one that went in and pulled the kids out of the house. There were no parents or other adults around; the kids had been left alone in the house and the place was really torched; there wasn't much left of it. We did double-time to Maryland General Hospital.

When we went into the facility, the docs took one look at the young boy and got him right to the treatment table. We put the young girl on a gurney and we stayed with her in the hallway. She was breathing alright, but she kept looking over her shoulder into the treatment area, where the docs were intubating and getting lines started on her brother. Eventually, they got him breathing again, and we had to get back on the road. As we were walking out of the treatment area to go back to the ambulance, this little girl, wearing nothing but a wet nightgown that was stained brown by the smoke, with a look of dismay in her eyes, turned her head and as I walked by said, "Merry Christmas, Mister." I will never forget hearing that. Here's a little child who's lost everything, her brother is in serious condition, and she took the time to thank me and wish me Merry Christmas, when I was just doing my job. It's one of the memories that'll stick with me forever, how this girl in her time of despair thought enough to wish me a Merry Christmas.

The following day, Christmas Day, we were at my in-laws' house, and I called the hospital to see how the boy was doing. My wife says, "This job is getting to you, it's just too much you know, that's not your problem, you do your job." And I guess she was hard about it, but it was interrupting her Christmas for five minutes. That stuff didn't happen that often, with my wife, but it does point out how some people don't really understand that you can't just turn off your concern when the day ends; you always carry your feelings and emotions with you.

One call we had for a shooting stands out. As we arrived, a woman was standing outside yelling, "Don't hurt my boy!" Two cops had started up the stairs, and my partner was in front of me following them. Since I knew the occupant, I yelled out, "Junior, where are you?" and I heard him reply from behind a door on my left. I turned the knob and pushed it open, and he was laying in the bed with a full body cast on, with a gun in his hand laying across his belly. I went into the room and could see that he was alright. However, sitting over in a nearby chair was the body of a woman who had obviously been shot in the head. Blood was all over the wall, and splattered all over the bed. As I walked in, I had my bag, so I went around the bottom of the bed and I put the bag on top of the gun, and then I said, "Let me have the gun, Junior." I put my hand under the bag and on top of the gun, and at that time my partner and the two police officers entered the room. Recognizing that it was a shooting, the officers drew their weapons. The first officer on the opposite side of the bed from me (a rookie), stuck his hand in and tried to grab the gun. The second officer took his nightstick and smacked the first officer, and told him to just back off. I was then able to pull out the gun and place it between Junior's legs where he couldn't reach it. There followed an educational session between the two officers, with one telling the other not to ever try manhandling a gun away. Junior admitted to shooting her, and when we asked her name, he said her name was "Bitch." He went to the hospital to get checked out, then right to jail. I'm sure he enjoyed being incarcerated in a full body cast.

Initially, we didn't get that many guns. Mostly we got razor blades or straight razors. Straight razors were a big deal and the victims often displayed their scars like a badge of honor. The guys had straight razors. The women would put blades between their fingers and slap each other.

It seemed at times that the perpetrators took great pleasure in slashing faces and abdomens, and it was not terribly uncommon to have protruding abdominal contents as well as numerous defense wounds on the victim. Knives and razors seemed to disappear from the scene as guns became an easier way of protecting individuals.

Another thing the women did, because we were near the waterfront, they would be unloading fertilizer down there a lot, and it was fish meal and it smelled terrible. So, the women would go in the backyard with a big pot of water and lye and wash the clothes. It was not that uncommon to see people with big, white splotches on them. A girl would have her boyfriend cheating, or her husband is out with someone else, and they would splash or throw lye on them. All we could do was to try to hose them down with whatever solutions we had on the vehicle. Upon arrival at the hospital, we would get a hose and hose out the back of the ambulance to try to dilute the caustic solution. Lye was readily available and this became a popular way of vengeance.

We even had one woman who bit another woman's titty nipple completely off.

Working out of the firehouse created some problems as the ambulance usually ran at a busy rate, and during the evening our leaving and returning was a big disturbance to the firefighters who were sleeping in anticipation of working their second jobs the following morning. I am not sure if it was our enjoying the street work or the moaning and groaning of the firefighters, but we most often found a way to stay on the streets all night.

While we were assigned to calls, we also had the ability to 'jump calls' by notifying the dispatcher that we were available for a call that had been assigned to another ambulance. This often would result in the dispatcher calling out a response on the radio, and waiting for one of the on-street ambulances to acknowledge that we would take it. One vehicle would then take the workload off of a neighboring unit. As the on-street unit was up and available, there was no need to awaken a neighboring unit, and no time was lost on the response.

We often would drop by dispatch with donuts or other comfort food for the dispatchers and enjoyed a good relationship with them. Our radio calls were often casual, "Ambo 1- Hey Lou can you guys take a call at 2200 W. Fayette for a cutting?" to which we would respond, "Got it covered, Willie." I am sure that would now be some violation of Department rules and probably the FCC as well.

One early evening we got called over to the penitentiary. We had to go through the sally port, where they open one gate and you go inside, then they close that gate and open another one in front of you. For a time, you stand in between the two gates. When the gates are opened and closed, lots of birds leave their perches on top. One of the newer guys was with me this time, so I asked him if he knew what kind of birds they were. He didn't, so I clued him in that they were jailbirds.

We went in to the kitchen, which was downstairs. The dining hall was upstairs, and the inmates used the dumbwaiters between the two to transport people as well as food. There's a guy stuck in one of the dumbwaiters, which were probably 34" across, 84" high and were stainless steel, side-by-side. The door to one is kind of bent out and this guy's leg was sticking out, and you could see the color was bad. He was trying to pull it out but only hurting himself more. Our first action was to try to jack the front sliding door away from the frame. Then we figured the best way to get access to him was from the dumbwaiter alongside him. At that time, we were wearing khakis, and this thing was filled with a greasy, grimy, yellow, filthy, slimy, dripping mess.

Anyway, I get inside the first one, and we started trying to open up the side of it so I could get into the second one. We get the sides pried up and I was able to sneak in there. He's really screaming so they start working on trying to push it off of the track a little bit. It wasn't working so well, so I yelled to the lieutenant to get me some oil. He turns around and tells one of the guards to get him some oil, and the guy comes back with a little can of 3-in-1 machine oil, which would have been suitable for oiling a sewing machine or door lock, but certainly not enough to accomplish what we needed to do. The lieutenant told him we wanted to oil the man, not the 'F-ing' clock, and he finally came back with a gallon of cooking oil.

After I oiled the kid up, some of the firefighters were putting pressure on the door to give us some space. The only way to get his leg out of there was to push it from the bottom and pull it from the top. He was now covered with oil, and the easiest way for me to bring his leg back into the dumbwaiter was to put my arms around him, have him put his arms around my neck, and then attempt to stand. I just told him to hang in there, and when I push up, for him to push up with his other leg, which was still in good shape. With the combination of the firefighters pushing on his foot from the bottom, and me getting into a standing position, we brought his leg back up into the dumbwaiter. At that time the rescuers below were able to rip the door off, and we lowered him out and took him to University Hospital. His leg was badly gnarled, and we had a time controlling the bleeding.

As they were checking him out, I was still in my filthy, oil-covered, bloody khakis. When we were leaving the hospital, he yelled something to get my attention and he says, "I never thought I'd say this to a honkey, but thanks." We did check later and heard they were able to save his leg. All that trouble just to avoid walking up a set of stairs!

One night in the middle of the night, all of a sudden we hear a civilian hollering, "Help! Help! Some dude got shot!" We climbed in the ambo and the reporting individual ran up the sidewalk and around the corner. My driver followed him up the sidewalk to where he stopped and pointed to a car. Unfortunately, my driver did not do an overall scene survey, and he pulled up and stopped the ambulance right next to an individual standing outside the driver's door of the car. The driver's window had been shot out, and a bullet round had been fired through the windshield as well. He pulled up within 2 feet of the individual standing outside the car, and I noticed that he had a gun in his hand. Unable to move until he pulled the ambo up, all I could see of the individual outside the car was that he had a strange look on his face, as if he were in shock or caught taken by surprise, as if he realized he was in a bad situation. I opened the passenger door of the ambulance, and told him to give me the gun, at which point he handed me the end of it. I opened the side door of the Edwards and put the gun in the oxygen cabinet, closing the side door. Looking in the car, I saw an individual that had been shot in the head but was moaning, slumped over to the passenger side.

I have often thought if I'd had a set of handcuffs, I would've cuffed this guy to the door of the car. However, the cops rolled in and he took off running into the park. We transported the gunshot individual (later found to be a cop) to a local hospital, where miraculously, he survived his injuries. After receiving a tongue lashing for taking the gun, and endangering myself and my partner, about two months went by and the victim of the shooting was recognized for his line of duty injury. He had been watching the shooter in relationship to a truck hijacking. Not only did the city recognize him, but myself and a well-known stripper of the day, Blaze Star, was also recognized at the same award ceremony. She was always going out of her way to open up the entertainment center of Baltimore City (comprised of numerous bars) to all the Vietnam vets for open bar and other festivities. Numerous Baltimore City police officers volunteered to be downtown as well, to keep the peace. That's the first and last time I had my picture taken with a world-renowned stripper.

Working downtown Baltimore put us in the area of many of the arenas and sports venues. Amongst the different programs we were able to cover for medical care was the Ringling Brothers, Barnum & Bailey Circus, which came to town virtually every year. One evening we had an individual who was attempting to cross the street and got hit by a transit bus. The injuries were extremely severe, but doing an assessment of the patient was very diffi-cult as we had no idea what language he spoke. This individual was alone and, as soon as we were able to figure out that he was with the circus, we sent the police down to the Civic Center to tell them we needed somebody that could speak whatever language the individual may be speaking. They were smart enough to get two or three different individuals that spoke their native languages as is commonly done in the circus made up of individu-als from numerous countries. We had someone that spoke German, and someone that spoke French and understood English as well, and ended up having a conversation as we were packing the patient for transport, where we asked the questions in English, someone spoke in another language, the other person then related to the victim and then the answers came back to us.

It was difficult and I'm not sure I would remember the languages that were used, but the end result was that we were able to get information from the victim and do an assessment.

During the holiday season firehouses used to decorate their quarters with lights and signs and holiday greetings. My partner and I both had Santa Claus hats which we would wear going into the hospital, but not on the street. The ambulances at that time had a muslin material which covered the rear windows. Somehow, we managed to get lace curtains made up for the back of the ambulance, and with an application of glass wax and detailing on the glass, we were able to decorate the sides and back windows of the ambulance. We also removed the red globe light from the cab and put decorations on it. It was not difficult for us to play a copy of jingle bells or another similar song on the PA system of the ambulance. We had a lot of fun doing it, until one day when we returned to quarters and the captain was standing at the head of the stairs and yelled for us both to get upstairs. We went up and received a severe tongue lashing for being disobedient and inappropriate. He then told us to clean it up. As we were removing the decorations from the ambulance, the captain appeared at the top of the stairs and yelled for the ambo crew again. We went back to meet the captain, only to be informed that we should put the ambulance back to its former festive condition, as the local newspaper, the Baltimore Sun, was sending photographers over. Evidently the general public thought it was a neat idea and called the newspaper, and we ended up on the front page of the newspaper. The captain was not pleased at all, but not another word was said. To the best of my knowledge, though, none of the other ambulance crews followed our lead.

Like all firefighters and medics, we supplemented our income with side jobs. One side job I had was hanging aluminum siding. I worked for an individual that had an after-hours milk bar, which was really a speakeasy, and we had been hanging siding the day before I went into work. Early the following morning we got a call for a shooting at the milk bar. When we went in, it was Gus – Gus who was my aluminum siding partner. He had been shot in the head, he was sitting leaned over the end of the bar and he said, "Hey Louie,

I'm not gonna die, am I?" I told him no, packaged him up and got him to the hospital, and he did survive. Months later, a new dispatcher for the Shock Trauma Unit and Medevac System came up to me and said, "You don't know who I am." I acknowledged I didn't, and she said, "Gus is my father." I found out later that she was also dating one of the medics that I worked with, and we became close friends. Small world.

I'll talk about a few memorable deliveries.

We went out on a call for a childbirth and got to the home, and it was a typical Baltimore City row home, a brick home about 13 feet wide, going from the main street out to the back alley. The houses were 2 stories, and then they all had an angled roof on it which we called a cockloft, which was supposed to be an attic. The attics usually had a small window in the front but the way they had built them was, they had knocked out the ceiling and put in a set of stairs going into the attic in order to give them extra living space. The side walls were probably 3 feet high, and then the roof angled on up. One of the dangers with these added-in rooms, was that when they put up the homes there was one common attic to run at least half the length of the houses in the block. Sometimes the whole way. They were a real firefighting hazard because once a fire broke through there and ran down those cocklofts, then you'd have smoke coming out every roof opening in the neighboring homes, right down the row. It was not uncommon to lose the roofs of 3 or 4 houses if you got a good burning fire. The call we got was for a childbirth. We went in and sure as heck we were led up into the second-and-a-half floor, or the cockloft, and were met by about 4 mattresses lying on the floor up there. No sheets or pillow cases or anything, just stained mattresses on the floor. There was a young girl, approximately 14 years old, that was in the middle of a delivery. The head was delivered out, but she didn't seem to be making much progress. This was my first live delivery in the field, and I knelt down on the mattress and checked the baby and she looked up at me and said, "Hey Mister, got a cigarette?" I told her we'd do the delivery first and then we'd both have a cigarette, which we did. We made the delivery, the baby was fine, we wrapped the baby up, and as my partner took the baby downstairs, she and I had a cigarette. Then I cleaned her up a bit and brought her down the narrow stairs as well. I don't know what became of the baby or the mother. But the delivery went smooth as the head had already been delivered.

Once we had a guy come running into the firehouse, and said his girl was having a baby. They lived only a block and a half from the fire station. So we went over and they were on the second floor, in the usual tenement type thing, small stairway with a turn in it, and we go up and she's on the bed, and I examine her and she's bulging but not fully crowning. There were 3 guys there as well. I said go and get the BOA kit, the 'born on arrival' kit. We had this little kit with scissors and a tie for the umbilical cord, a bulb syringe to clean out the kid's mouth and all. So I said, "It's gonna be a little bit, and I don't wanna get you in that stairway and have to bend your kid to get him out." She laughed, she was good about it. Because they lived so close to the firehouse, they had walked by a lot and they were familiar with us; they were just kids themselves. So we mentioned that we had been watching the Stanley Cup playoffs, and said laughingly should we go back to the station, we have enough time to finish the game and then come back later to deliver the baby. The guy says, "You don't need to do that," and he wheels in a portable TV on a stand and sets it up. So I called for the snorkel to come up to the window, so when we delivered the baby we would put them out the window and send them down to the ambulance and to the hospital rather than going all the way around. So the snorkel comes, and I explain to them that we've got a delivery in progress, and they're gonna need to take her out the window. So they got the snorkel up at the window, and we turned the TV so that they could see as well. There were 2 guys in the snorkel watching, and we watched the playoffs as well from inside. We ended up, after she delivered, taking her down the stairs anyway.

Another strange delivery we had was for a preemie, and as we went into the house, we took a look and here was this length of, what looked like a loaf of burned bread, that had been delivered by this young girl. I was amazed when we looked at it that it wiggled and moved and everything. So we naturally started working on it quickly, and we called for another ambulance because we had access to what we called a preemie carrier, but it was always kept in the engine house, or the station. The best way of describing it was an aluminum toolbox with a sling inside and slots on the bottom. We were to fill rubber hot water bottles and put them in the sleeves, and that was what was to provide the heat for the baby. We had one for the foot, both sides, and the floor of the box. And then the baby would hang in a hammock above it. For oxygen, we had a small funnel that attached to an oxygen tank on the outside and we put liter flow oxygen inside the container with the child and we'd run like hell for the hospital. Not unlike the dog and cat carriers we have today, these aluminum things weighed quite a bit, but that's what we had in the older days.

The last experience with childbirth I'll talk about was more than average in that it happened later in my career, when I had 3 children at home, the youngest being 8 months old. We had experienced a number of miscarriages and were anxious to have more children. We had a call approximately 7 in the morning, so I had a firefighter driving the ambulance, and strangely enough the call was right across the street from a small religious hospital and about 3 blocks from Johns Hopkins hospital, which had a world-renowned unit called Harriett Lane. Harriett Lane was a separate building attached by a maze of tunnels to the main hospital.

When we went in the house, I discovered a newborn in distress and called my partner into the bathroom, where the delivery had taken place. As I mentioned we did not carry on board the ambulance anything special for children other than an air bulb syringe to clear the airway and nasal passages. I told him to get something to wrap the child in, and he brought me a pillow case after shaking the pillow out of it that he had found on a couch in the adjacent room. We were so close, and because the baby had been born so blue, requiring a few puffs of mouth-to-mouth to get him started breathing, I was looking at the time factor it would take to get into a medical facility. I grabbed the baby and placenta and headed for the ambo, and jumped in the front passenger seat holding the infant. I got on the radio and told dispatch to notify Hopkins that we were coming in with a newborn in distress, and to please have the pediatric staff from Harriett Lane meet us in the adult emergency room. The reason I did that rather than going over to Harriett Lane is, we had no voice communications with them and for security purposes they had a watchman that controlled gates going in and out of there, and I knew it would be a real delay. We also didn't know the layout of the emergency room of Harriett Lane, and felt it would be much better to meet them in a facility that we knew and where they could get all their equipment quickly. The little boy was immediately received by the Harriett Lane staff and they took him back into the treatment area and removed the placenta. After gathering what information we could, I turned to look for the mother and was surprised to hear that she had ridden in, in the back of my ambulance. I had completely forgotten any of her needs as I was focused on the infant. I was told that she had been taken upstairs and the doctors had determined that this would be the last child that she needed to have, as she was undergoing a hysterectomy. So while we were in the back dealing with the newborn, the doctors had apparently examined her and sent her upstairs to be next in line for surgery.

Remember these are the older days, and that child was adopted, and my wife and I had custody of him at 10 days. I contacted my lawyer, and the social workers at the hospital, and we had the temporary adoption lined up that quickly. This was really close to a miracle, as if the state had taken control of the child, he would have gone into a foster home. We certainly would not have been eligible with already having 3 children, and with having one of them only 8 months old. He came out of the hospital and has been with us ever since. We were able to adopt him after explaining the situation to the judge.

We arranged a meeting with the mother, and the social worker from the hospital was involved as well as the registration clerk and all that, and I brought our book of photos of us on vacations, and we told her look, we can give him a life that he'll never have otherwise. The state had already taken 2 girls away from her. My wife and I went up to talk with the mother, and she said she'd be willing to sign him over to us, so we didn't have to go through the state. It was a private adoption type of thing. The following day we went downstairs and the lady at the desk knew me and my partner, and the judge had drawn up the papers for us, and the social worker joined my wife and me and the mother of the baby, still in her bed, and she had to sign the papers and the social worker had to witness it, and everybody in the room was crying. It was a pretty heartwarming thing. I think my wife was happy that she had another baby without having to sleep with me.

Bringing him home added a second boy to our family of 4 that went girl/ boy/girl/boy. We were blessed to have the pieces fall in place, and of course the fire department took advantage of this adoption and I ended up getting an award from the mayor and front-page coverage in the newspaper. My wife, on the other hand, told me in no uncertain terms that I could not make a habit of bringing children home.

Over the years I delivered something like 18 children. Unfortunately, most of these were children being born to children, serving the inner city and having a large number of single mothers in that society at that time. Most of these children were raised in high-rise buildings operated by the government and, just to clarify there were terms used as high-rise jungles, and open-air prisons, etc. The buildings were usually built in a u-shape or a square shape facing each other with an inner courtyard that had access doors, stairways and elevators, and in the middle was a small plot of grass that virtually never turned green because of all the traffic and activity that took place in there, from basketball to bike riding etc. When it rained it was a mud pit. It didn't take me long after dealing with some of the kids in there, and when I say kids I mean from 5 on up, it didn't take much to gather a bunch of kids when the ambulance pulled up. We would always have a mob around us, and on occasion when we left the ambulance to go up in the high rise, they would find their way in and snatch this or the other thing. I found it very easy to convince the kids that we were there to help somebody, and that they could help us, and usually by giving them a task to help us, such as pulling the stretcher in, running ahead and getting the elevator ready for us, carrying the aid bag or a handful of 4x4s and telling them to stick with us, it made them feel special and the rest of the group was not as interfering with us, they'd have a path cleared for us and so on.

An additional thing was that the kids rode the tops of the elevators. They'd pry the doors open, quite ingeniously, with a coat hanger that they had bent and kept in the incinerator chute on each floor so they could snag a door, open it up, and then just get on the roof of the elevator car and operate it from there. The first couple of times that happened when we got there, we'd get in the elevator and we didn't even have to push the button, you could yell to the kid, "We're going to 7" and the elevator would move and stop at the floor, and the doors would open for us, and out we'd go. It was almost like having a permanent attendant. Surprisingly in my time with the ambulance service, I only encountered one incident where they stopped us between floors and we were kind of trapped in the elevator. We beat and banged on the doors as they laughed and jumped up and down on the top of the car. They had us trapped and trapped good. It's interesting that we never had any of the kids injured. This was their internal playground and in all the years we never had a kid injured in the elevator shafts.

There was one exception and that was the night we got a call, we went in, 'man fell in the elevator' was the call. The elevator was in the basement area giving us access to just walk in and they had the doors open already, and the remains of the victim were obvious to us. Shortly thereafter the police and fire units arrived and helped us move the victim's remains after taking pictures. We were called back to the scene about 3 am by the police investigators and went up to the 7th floor. As we got off the elevator on the 7th floor, naturally the doors closed and the police officers finished their interviews with the rest of the gang that was involved with the victim. We went to get on the elevator and the elevator wouldn't come, though we heard kids' voices in it, so the officers took their clipboards and tried to pry the doors back, and couldn't do it. Until a 7- or 8-year-old watching said, "You want the door open, mister?" and we said yeah, and that's when we found out they were keeping their homemade 'keys' in the refuse chutes that ran down to the incinerator in the basement. But to see this kid, like Harry Houdini pull out his 'key' and open the door for these 2 ambulance crew members and 6 or so police officers there, everybody was turning their heads in disbelief. I don't know why it took us so long to figure out how they were getting in there, but as long as they were serving us and helping us, we had no problems with it.

Even during the 1968 riots we had no problems with our ambulance being harassed or put into a feeling of danger in the high rises, as the kids, many of whom had grown up with us in and out the building, for one reason or another seemed to protect our ambulance. It was easy for them to know who it was as the ambulance had large numbers on the roof and they could tell it was us responding. The projects created major problems for others, firefighters, police and ambulance crews, but we encountered the minimum interference and till today I still believe it was because we took the time to assure that we gave them no reason to distrust us.

The riots started in the south, moved up the east coast and there was no doubt, we all knew that our turn was coming. One lieutenant was almost like the weather man, charting the progress of the civil unrest up the east coast and figured that within an hours' timeframe that the first of it would break out nearby in a specific area of the city. And as everyone else was watching and listening we found out that somehow, he knew where the first outbreak would be and he pegged it right on the button, down on Gay and Orleans streets. The community in which the riots were conducted was well aware of what was happening, and their homes and businesses and lives were in danger, and the way they protected it was, they would either paint in the windows 'black owned' or hang black flags outside. Nailing a rag on the door was seen as a way of protecting their property from everything. Of course, we had black members of the department and ambulance service that were caught in the middle of this civil disobedience, as well as police officers of color being, I believe, targeted even more so than the white officers. It's a time that I remember but also a time I hope I never see again, where a community turns on itself. It never made sense to me to have these businesses, black and white and Asian, burned to the ground when there were no other resources to serve the community as this progressed.

We had the National Guard come in, ride around in jeeps and put barbed wire across some of the streets, but for the most part I think the riot burned itself out. There was very little conflict as these kids all knew where they were going and trust me, most of the rioters were kids 20 or under, but they knew the buildings, the alleys, the rooftops and so on, and we had a bunch of National Guard personnel riding around with weapons; however, the word was they had no ammunition. Those looters and others that the police or National Guard could arrest were held in the Civic Center, and we made frequent trips down there to check on sick or injured people who wanted out of this bullpen of humanity.

During the riots where rowhouses were, alley apples (bricks) were flying like crazy. Remember, all these houses had brick chimneys and most of them were all dry. All you had to do was shake them and the bricks would come off. And the cops couldn't catch you because you could go from one house to the other to the other, drop down through a cockloft and start laughing. Some of our vehicles had National Guardsmen riding in them. We all pretty well stayed there around the clock for about 4 or 5 days.

Another interesting experience was one afternoon for an apparent heart attack, we found a 40-year-old male in cardiac arrest. We worked him as we did in those days, with CPR and the bag/valve mask with O2 and ran him to one of the local hospital ERs. The staff worked on him, and then pronounced him. The problem was, this was the first day that the new interns had been turned loose in the ER on their own. Most of you who have been in this service will have already experienced the fact that when the new doctors come in and take over, they're full of book learning and don't have much practical experience in dealing with the numerous situations they will encounter. The nurse informed the doctor that he should notify the family and he hesitantly started out to the waiting area. We were with him because we had to get patient information for our run reports. His approach was one I'll never forget. In that he walked into the waiting area with all the families, and asked if the 'Wilson Family' was there. Immediately an elderly woman (the grandmother), and the wife stood up, and a couple of children, and they all rushed in front of the doctor for information. The doctor looked at them and said, "Guess who died?" And that was the end of his statement. This was a young fellow that obviously had no people experience and he was known for a long time as Dr. Guess Who. And the word spread amongst the ambulance crews and some of the nursing staff as well. I'm sure he was counseled, but we just couldn't believe anyone could be so callous as to announce the death of a family member by saying, "Guess who died?"

Although we were paid by the fire department and spent our down time in their quarters, we formed an allegiance-working relationship with the Baltimore City Police Department. At this time in the downtown area we still had numerous walking posts for the police officers to get them close to the community (or to punish them, I'm not sure) but there were very few cars with partners in them. Each had a district and they used their district boundaries to the best of their ability. We had our numerous street people, homeless and a fair amount of no-goodniks, that roamed in gangs preying on visitors and individuals after dark, causing a number of injuries in these street crimes. During those days there were far fewer guns being used, as the weapon of choice was the straight razor. We collected many, many razors because they would usually be left at the scene. Remember this is before the days of DNA. We dealt with far more cuts than we did gunshot victims. We saw the increase over the years but never believed it would get to be as common as it is today. Usually the lacerations would be on the arms, abdomen or face of the victim, and those that were involved in less-than-legal activities were for some reason proud of the facial cuts and so on that they had received, and their scars were looked upon as signs of their experiences, not unlike the tattoos that quite often indicate gang memberships. They wouldn't hide their battle scars; they would wear them proudly.

While the 'cuttings' as they were called, and the numerous stabbings most often left injured victims, we did have gunshots and other fatalities where a body was obviously a fatality or a serious injury that couldn't be delayed transport. We worked very closely with the police in these instances, and on numerous occasions would chalk the body outline of the victim before the police arrived. We also did this at vehicle accidents, marking the four corners of each vehicle, for on occasion they'd start the vehicle and leave the scene before the police got there, and the accident investigation people had no clue as to what was going on prior to their arrival. I carried a large piece of white chalk in my turnout coat along with a few other tools of the trade such as a plastic squirt bottle full of ammonia, which we used to wake up patients and which also proved on occasion to be a deterrent to dogs and violent patients. Usually squirting the industrial strength ammonia from shoulder to breast-bone up to the other shoulder, forming a half-horse-collar of ammonia would cause a patient/victim/assailant to throw their head back and lose track of where you were, and no matter what way they turned their head they were in a cloud of ammonia. It cleared pretty quickly but usually allowed us time to physically restrain a patient. And another use was in the high-rises. Every second or third unit had a dog, and these dogs would bark at anybody walking down the hallway, so as we went down if there was a barking dog, we'd just put a squirt across the bottom of the door and it would filter inside and it would shut the dogs down from barking to whining, and keep them back in their rooms. It was a great deterrent. Not mace or pepper spray which we weren't allowed to carry, but we were allowed to carry ammonia to awaken patients.

The chalking of bodies prior to moving them was done for a number of reasons, but mostly to make sure that if we moved the body, the police knew exactly how it was laying and so on. However, the urge to put eyes, a nose and a smiling face on the drawing was one we had to overcome. We never did that, but we did do fingers sometimes, and THIS SIDE UP. We were called one afternoon to a liquor store and when we arrived there was a gentleman outside jumping up and down and yelling, "I didn't do it! I didn't do it!" We had no idea what he didn't do, until we entered and saw the owner of the liquor store laid out on the floor with an obvious gunshot to the head and the gun laying behind the counter. We figured that this 'guy that didn't do it' would have used his energy running down the street if he had actually been the perpetrator. As we were looking at the patient, he said the owner had just gotten a new gun and was showing it to him, and he said he walked out of the store and started to the corner and he heard the gunshot go off, and he came back and the gun had 'probably' gone off by itself as the man was unfamiliar with it. The man being so recently shot had a potential of survival, and for some reason I used a black magic marker from a display that was on the counter to mark his body, and we picked him up and took him to the hospital. He didn't survive. However, I got a call back about a week later from the business owner's son, who was reopening and when we arrived, he asked what the marking on the floor was for. I looked and realized that the magic marker had gone into the tile floor and I could see where they had tried to scrape it off, but the imprint was still there. That's the last time I used magic marker, but his question was what was it that we used, and I'm sure he ended up retiling over that before he reopened the store.

One Sunday we got a call to confirm a deceased patient. The streets were clear and quiet until we approached the house, which was on a corner. This was in a very affluent neighborhood. There was a crowd around the building and we didn't realize what we had, as most times you don't until you see it with your own eyes, but no one was up close to the building, on the porch or anything, and as we approached we got a strong odor which turned out to be chicken shit or poop coming from the house. It smelled like bird feathers or something. The cops were laughing as we went up and asked them what we had, and one said, "Go in the living room and you'll see." They watched us as we walked down the hallway, through the kitchen to the living room, and there was a deceased woman in there obviously with rigor mortis and the start of decomposition. But the smell was not coming from her alone. The furniture, the cabinetry, the kitchen table, the floor, everything was covered with newspaper as if someone would be getting ready to paint the ceiling or something, but we found out it wasn't. Because the place was loaded with chickens, free-range chickens in the house, not in cages. There were probably 30 chickens that were taken out of there by city animal control. We opened as many doors and windows as we could and went outside and awaited their arrival. After the chickens were gone, the medical examiner was called and he removed the body. It was just strange that here was this lady living in such a beautiful home with Victorian furniture and everything, and she had all those chickens in her house. And there was no sign outside of any chicken coops or anything.

Another unusual call was to an accident in the early evening and when we pulled up, we saw a taxi cab had been involved in an accident with another vehicle at an intersection. As we got out of the ambulance, we could hear this woman screaming, "That jitterbug son of a bitch M----- F-----!" She was a passenger in the right-hand side rear. I looked in and there was a woman, who had nothing worse than a bloody nose, and she was screaming and carrying on. Her screeches were unbelievable and she kept hollering about the 'G-- D---- jitterbug,' etc., and after calming her down I said, "Look lady, you're OK." And she said, "I'm not OK. We weren't stopped rolling before that jitterbug reached in and took my G-- D--- wig!" Apparently, some of the kids on the corner had seen the accident occur and saw the window down, reached in and snatched this woman's wig and headed on down the road with it.

Another time we ran into a wig was when a car hit a stone wall outside a school yard. There had been 4 or 5 passengers, and we were the second ambulance in. Being a school yard and a school day, we had our usual crowd of looky-loos. As we walked past the other ambulance crew, they were pulling the stretcher to their ambulance with a patient, and we asked what we had, and their response was, "Front seat." We went up to the passenger door and looked in, and on the dashboard was a wig. As the windshield had been broken out, we didn't know if we had a patient's scalp and she had been pulled out or what, until we grabbed the edges of it and lifted it up and saw a label on the back of it.

Responding to a call once, the kitchen door was open, and we went in. There was a woman there with a knife on the table in front of her, and she had blood on her apron and her hands so we knew we had a cutting. We started with her, asking if she was alright because we didn't know if she had cut her arms or we had an attempted suicide or something. And she said,

"He's in there," so we turned and looked in the living room, and here's a male who has been severely cut, stabbed and slashed, and he's lying on half of the daybed. We went in and checked him, and there was no doubt he was dead. So we called for the police, and we told her to just sit down, and I grabbed the knife and pulled it across the table away from her, and she offered no resistance, no problems whatever. She apparently had solved her problems with this gentleman. So we began our wait for the police to come, but it was Sunday and we had just purchased our lunches, so my partner went down to the ambo and brought our subs up, and he sat down on the other end of the daybed, and I sat at the table keeping an eye on her. We expected the police to be there quick on a Sunday morning. So we started eating our subs, but here's my partner next to this body all chewed up, just eating his sandwich, and the cops came stomping up the stairs, turned and as soon as they saw it they said, "You G-- D--- guys!" as they apparently weren't used to seeing that. They didn't have the stomachs that we did, weren't tough guys like us. They called for the medical examiner who came up and confirmed that this gentleman had been sliced and diced and was, in fact, deceased.

Once, we weren't even on a call, we were just leaving a hospital, and as we made our turn there was a brawl going on spilling off the sidewalk into the street. There were 2 sides to it which was quite obvious because you had a number of blacks working together and a number of whites working together, that seemed intent on killing each other. The bar must have emptied out because there must have been 30-40 people involved, and as we pulled down, my partner stopped the vehicle and we called in that we were at that location for a disturbance, figuring that a couple of yells for them to knock it off would calm the situation. But it didn't, so I grabbed the radio and I called headquarters and told them to get the police out here immediately, we had a signal 40 which was our code for ambulance needs assistance. The dispatcher comes back, over the loud speaker, "Ambulance 1, what do you need the police for?" So the whole crowd hears this, and my response to the dispatcher was, "Because we've got people fighting out here, and barstools in the air, and we need a signal 40." So the police arrived and they came in, and with them came some of the plainclothes officers, and their cars came in from everywhere, and they started pulling people apart, and one kid was running from one of the plainclothes police officers, and in the sidewalk, every few feet there was no sidewalk there. There was dirt where the city had planted little trees, but the little trees usually lasted about a week before the kids ripped them out and threw them in the street, or whatever. But the policeman was chasing this kid and he reached out for him and the kid stepped into one of those things, twisted his ankle and went over. He ended up breaking his ankle. So besides them breaking up the fight (people had their belts off, were swinging them at each other, etc.), they took about 6 of them to jail, and one group started trying to say it was police brutality, breaking this kid's ankle. And fortunately, the officer was black as well as the kid.

So we got called into court, and the judge lined up all of the kids, and now I'm saying kids, but these people were our age and older, just has them all lined up, and we're sitting in our seats and everything, and the judge says, "What happened?" so we said, "We came around the corner and this was going on, this guy had his belt off and was swinging it around, …" so the judge said something about "When will people stop all this black and white crap? You know what I wish? I wish I'd wake up one morning and everybody would be grey." I thought that was kind of cool. So then he read off the names. And the main kid that was there hitting people with his belt, his sister kept saying he didn't even have a belt on that night, here's his belt, she brought it in, and it was home that night. And so the judge looks on the list, and he calls, "J. Wilson." J. Wilson steps forward, and the judge says, "No, step back, I'll get to you." Then he calls the next name, who steps forward and gets sentenced. In between each of the others, he calls J. Wilson to step forward, then tells him, "No, no step back, I'll get to you." He waited until the end to deal with J. Wilson. I think he got 2 years. The cop involved stopped by the firehouse every now and then, and when Evel Knievel made his jump over Snake River Canyon I was working at the Civic Center, and I brought my son with me, and he sat with this cop. He thought it was so great to be able to sit with a homicide detective.

On one call, my partner and I went to one of the flophouses, and got in this little old elevator that had a door that closed, but it was just a gate door. We went up and it was for an overdose. So the guy that watches the desk says, "Room so-and-so" and that's all he says. So we go up and as you go in the room there are some people outside in the hallway, and we go in and here's this decent looking chick in bed, and the room is full of all these boas, so she was obviously a stripper, and the eyelashes on the side table, looked like spiders, and she had all the fancy clothes and everything in there. We tried to wake her up and she didn't come around, and in those days, we didn't have any narcan or anything to combat the drugs. So we brought the stretcher in, but we couldn't get it in to the elevator because of the legs on it, so we went back out and got the stokes basket, because that's solid and you can lift it up, hold it vertical. So, we went up to the room and got her in the stokes basket, the police were there, they helped us get it down. We get her in the elevator, stood the stokes basket up – we couldn't lay it down in the elevator, had it lifted up, and held onto her, brought her down put her on the stretcher, took her out of the building and took her over to the hospital. So the doctor says, "I'm gonna intubate her." (That means you pull her head back and put a tube down her throat.) And as he grabs hold he says, "Damn, she's got a beard." And my partner was standing at the foot of the stretcher, picks up the sheet and says, "She's got a beard down here, too." And the nurse laughs and then we hear this other voice, but it's obviously a male voice, hollering, "Where is so-and-so", and around the corner comes this other drag queen. One of the Hopkins sex changes. They used to all hang out over near the bus terminal. Because we were by there often on our way in and out of the hospital, we'd wave and they'd wave back to us, "Hi Sweetheart!" "How's my honey?" etc.

Behind the firehouse was a parking area and then another place called the Wild Indian, and it was a place for the hippies where they bought the fancy clothes and all that stuff. We were out in the lot one day and I started talking to this kid, and I think he was Indian, like a Pakistani Indian, and we just were shooting the shit about being a fireman and all that. Another day he comes around and says, "We got a problem." I asked what the problem was and he said, "We got a girl, we're not sure if she's overdosed or what but we can't have her in the building anymore." She was a runaway, probably 15 or 16 years old. And runaways don't do well when you return them to where they ran away from. So I went over there and we talked and she wasn't overdosed, but she was a little dopey and he said she couldn't stay there because of the business and everything. I said, "Look, I ain't here to harass anybody, you guys are all right as long as I'm concerned." We had parking privileges in the parking garage. And we'd drive in, park our own cars, then get on the dolly. (They had a belt with steps on it, and you just stepped on the thing and hold the next step and the belt would take you down. As someone went up, you'd be on the other side.) They had a little office in the front and they had an electric heater in there, and what they did was in trade for us taking care of the place at night, they'd bring over their little fishing tackle box with the keys and the tickets, and people would give us their tickets and we'd give them their keys. They would have pulled all the cars down near the first floor so people didn't have to do that. And it was a nice little trade off, nice to be able to park there. But we also had keys to their little office. So I told him to bring her down the firehouse around 6:00 that night. So they came around the corner into the firehouse, and what we did was, we gave her blankets or jackets or whatever, because there were concrete floors in there. We opened it up and turned the heater on and let her stay in there, and then about 4:30 or 5 in the morning we'd go over and wake her up and she'd go back around to the place. And she was there for probably 2 or 3 weeks. And she didn't create any trouble, steal anything, or come across and start messing with the firemen. After she was gone, I didn't know where she went or whatever, she just kind of disappeared. This Indian kid comes walking on down, and he's got a pair of pants hanging over his shoulder. And the pants were a dark brown, they had a yellow stripe down the side like the US Cavalry, it was yellow and it had all embroidered flowers in it, all the way down and they were hip huggers with a bell bottom. And he said, "These are for you, thanks for helping her out." And I put them on and they fit. Of course, I was not the hippie type at that time, but they fit and everything. I thought that was neat that they did that.

Lot of times we had people come by with cookies or something, not as much downtown as out there in Highlandtown. When we got a call over to the west side of town, and were leaving from the station, the guys would always tell us to grab them a cone from the ice cream place, so when we finished the call we'd grab some cones. They didn't have any holders or anything. After one call, we drop the patient off at Franklin Square, and we stop and get the ice cream, and my partner's driving and I've got these 4 cones in my hands. And it seems like we can't get back across town fast enough, and all these cones are all melting down my hands, all over my lap and everything. I had to change my clothes and all, and these guys were all hollering, "That ain't an ice cream cone!" So they were all upset, but fortunately they'd given me the money for the cones.

Once a year the chief of the department comes around unannounced and does inspections at the firehouse. So we had no idea he was coming. We were over on the west side where the dog pound was, and we were just kind of killing time, and I said, "Let's go down to the pound." I'd never been there before. And the door was open, the guy let us walk through, and it's like any other pound, it smells like poop, it's damp because they hose everything out, the dogs are all scraggly, and I'm walking through and all of a sudden it seemed like there was a little rag in a back corner, and I look and it's shivering and shaking and everything, and the guy says, "Yeah, they're gonna be put down," and I asked, "What about that one?" and he opens up the door and brings it out. It was little with black and white stripes. So I said, "You can't put that one down; how much is he?" and he says, "It's a she, and they don't have a price on these 'cause they're gonna put 'em down." I said, "What do I have to do, to get one?" And he says, "Pffft." So we got back in the ambulance and went back to quarters, stationed downtown, and there were 2 beds upstairs where we slept, and you came out and down the stairs and we had a bathroom right down there at the bottom of the stairs and the ambulance parked right there. So, we were separated a bit, and I took the dog in the bathroom and I put him in the sink and I start washing him off, and all of a sudden, the gong goes off – the chief is here for the inspection.

So he's going through all the trucks and stuff outside, but I know he's headed to us and I don't know what I'm gonna do with the dog. There's no shower to lock it up or anything. So I'm wiping him off with paper towels, because I didn't want to use real towels, and I'm all wet too from washing him. So when the chief stepped into our little area, I just stood outside the bathroom, had the door closed, and I'm thinking "Don't wimper, don't yelp," and I'm all wet, and the chief says, "Jordan, how you doing?" I said, "Yeah I'm just cleaning up some stuff around here," and he didn't go in the bathroom or anything, he walked around and walked out. I don't know what kind of trouble I would have gotten in. That was the day of the year where they set an example. They had to find something wrong, a cracked glass in the window. I had my uniform on but it was soaking wet. This was when I was working at the fire department and at shock trauma.

One of the important aspects of the ambulance service as far as I'm concerned, was not the fire department's involvement in it, but what the hospital's involvement with it was.

We found that over a short period of time, we were incorporated into the initial care of patients being brought into the facility. We would tell them our report, what we had determined had happened to the patient, help them move the patient, and on numerous occasions would assist their staff in getting a patient to x-ray or cleaning a wound or whatever. So, our skills developed over a period of time. It started to become apparent that there was more that we would be able to do, that would be helpful to the doctors, nurses and the patient, that could be done before we got there. Eventually they started expecting more from us before we got there. I enjoyed what they were doing and did have a thirst for more knowledge and capabilities. At the hospital, a lot of the nursing and physician staff would encourage us to take part in what was going on, so it was a two-way learning experience.

Later a national document, the White Paper on Trauma came out. That study showed that your odds of being properly cared for in an emergency were minimal, and that a large number of ambulance services were in fact being run by funeral parlors. I believe somewhere it stated that you had a 50-50 chance of being picked up by a hearse. There were instances where it was reported that, going to a multi victim accident, it would not be all that uncommon for a deceased victim to be picked up and taken to the funeral parlor, or to the city morgue, or to the hospital, because the body would not be released until payment was made. And the injured party that was taken to a hospital may not be as easy to collect from, so there was a mercenary overtone to it, and this is a story that permeated the EMS field. After the White Paper on Trauma came out, a number of physicians and government authorities saw what a disgrace this was to the citizens, and efforts were made to improve.

SHOCK TRAUMA CENTER

Undoubtedly, one of the most important experiences in my career has been my involvement with the Shock Trauma Unit in Baltimore, at one of the hospitals that I routinely went to with patients, the University of Maryland Hospital in downtown Baltimore. Being on the ambulance and in and out of the emergency room, we quickly formed a close relationship with the nursing staff who were pleased to utilize our capabilities, as they were one of the busiest facilities. We also got to know the attending physicians as well as interns. While they ran what I would consider, and still consider, a very good operation, they were often burdened with more than enough patients to keep them working, and our assistance was welcomed. We all got to be on a first-name basis, and in those days, we could have our dispatcher notify them via phone that we were coming in with a seizure, cutting etc. This allowed them to prepare for us and our reports to them, and allowed them to prepare for any critical patients coming in. In those days, they were the highest level of care available. There were very few specialty units as we know them now, so they handled virtually everything, and those that they couldn't handle in the ER were quickly shuffled to the ORs or specialty areas to be attended to by other doctors.

One that introduced himself to me, by the name of Dr. R Adams Cowley, was a heart surgeon that had more vision than any physician I've ever met. He had been told to talk to me by someone on the nursing staff at University Hospital. He invited me up to his unit, which at that time was two beds and was known as the 'Death Lab.' Dr. Cowley made it clear that he was not satisfied that we collectively were not treating people as we should be. He pointed out that one of the major problems was that by the time a patient had worked himself up the ladder of severity, too much time had been lost, and there was virtually no way to catch up. Dr. Cowley had spent time with the military and had seen firsthand how care from the top-down, not bottom-up, and having the proper people and facilities available to minimize the devastating effects of injuries, could greatly improve the outcome.

At that first meeting, Dr. Cowley made it clear that if we needed him, or if a patient needed his unit, that he would be more than happy to accept any patients we brought in from the street. Dr. Cowley took me through the unit introducing me to the other individuals there, and then said that if we needed the unit, to bring the patient right to him. He gave me the phone number, because we were not connected, and I wrote it in magic marker on the top of the ambulance stretcher pad. I also gave the number to headquarters. Up until then, we always took patients to the emergency room, but now I could call dispatch and tell them not to call the regular number, but to call this number and tell them we're coming in, and to meet us downstairs.

The first patient that I brought in was an Oriental gentleman who had been crossing the street. He was right in front of a bus when the light changed, and had suffered what we referred to as total body crunch. We were only about four blocks from the hospital. I had the driver hand me the mic, and I told the dispatcher that we were going in to the trauma unit and to use their number, and when we arrived, they were downstairs waiting for us. We went right down the hallway onto the elevator and to the second floor. We helped strip the patient and stood back as the team of doctors and nurses in the admitting area attended to him. Later that afternoon, I got a call from my battalion chief asking who the hell I thought I was, that he sets the standards, etc., etc. I contacted Dr. Cowley, who was livid, and he told my chief that he was a doctor, and he'd given me those directions, and that if he had a problem with it, that they could have a meeting and get it worked out.

From that point on, we started bringing seriously injured patients directly to the trauma unit. Dr. Cowley said thanks to me for making the right decision, and said we needed more right decisions being made. We talked at length about his visions for the future, and he asked about what EMTs needed to provide better care. Dr. Cowley felt we could integrate the EMT skills with the trauma unit through the ambulance service. Here was a well-known doctor talking to a young firefighter-EMT, asking my opinions. This made me realize that if change came, he would be on the forefront.

Over time, protocols were developed and people felt more comfortable that ambulance crews were following those protocols to determine where to bring or send patients. Battalion chiefs wouldn't stand in the way.

I had recently been fortunate to be selected as an initial instructor for the EMT program. He asked me if I'd consider working with him and the ambulance companies, and offered me a position at the trauma unit. There was no hospital position for an EMT in 1972, so he hired me as a unit technician. I took the job, and the opportunity to work there part-time working around my EMT training duties and my fire department shiftwork, which I kept up full-time until 1973.

Staff was made up of in-house trauma staff of virtually all specialties. We ended up, over time, having not only our old military supplies but expensive Emerson/Engstrom respirators to use, and other costly equipment that did not have to be gathered up and brought to the patient's side. The patient would come from the street to a mini-operating room, separated only by glass windows with the OR nurses standing inside and waiting for the patient to arrive for whatever medical care was deemed necessary. There's no sense telling most of you readers what a hectic situation it could be when you rolled up with a critical patient and the place you went to wasn't geared up and waiting for the arrival of the patient.

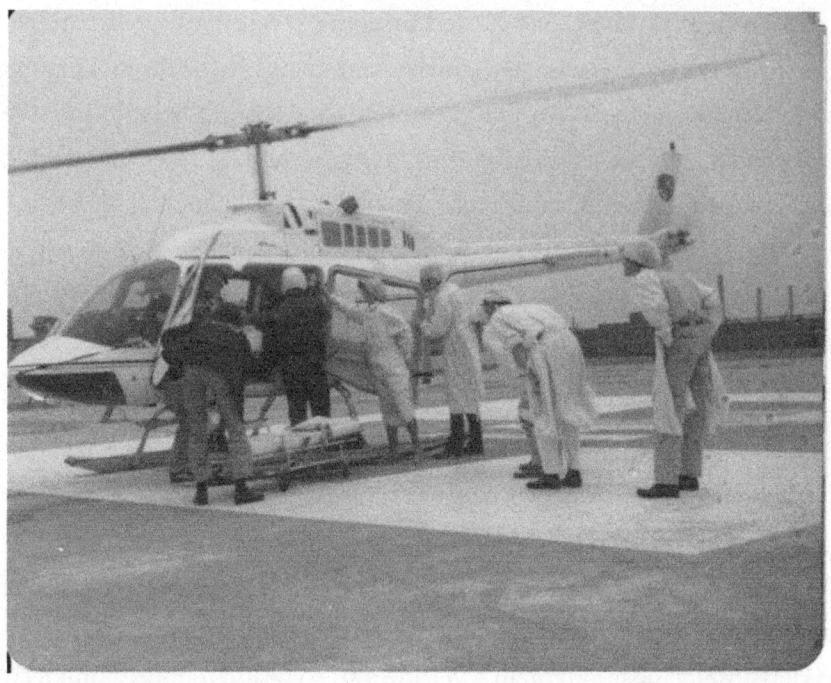

At the Shock Trauma Unit, an A-Team was there all the time; there was no calling doctors in and waiting for them to arrive. Over time, I was trained to assist the trauma team in giving initial care. They saw that I could assist in speeding up some of the processes, also saving more qualified individuals to do higher-level care. The nurses and doctors helped me expand my knowledge under their watchful eye, training me on techniques not used on the ambulance, such as inserting Foleys, splinting, monitoring abdominal lavage (belly tap) results and transfusions, restraining patients and running to the blood bank. Later I was taught intubation at the main hospital. I worked with LPNs and applied to the American Association of Physician's Assistants, documenting my experiences with the Shock Trauma staff, and received my PA certification. PAs were fairly new at the time.

The Unit grew from 2 beds to 4. Campus security police looked the other way as we filled midnight requisitions from the gymnasium, but the unit was gaining too much notoriety. The hospital shut us down. The ORs were off limits to the trauma unit. So we planned to move patients out, and let the press know about it. The Arbutus Fire Department offered to help us out with transport. Begrudgingly, the hospital then agreed to let us use their ORs and other resources.

The trauma unit was growing in recognition; however, a number of hospitals were hesitant to send patients to the trauma unit because of the financial loss when they transferred the patient. I remember Dr. Cowley objecting to this, and I heard him on many occasions state that a man should not live or die based on his wallet or ability to pay. And I saw this in practice, such as when you brought in a patient who had been shot, and also a patient who was the shooter. Each individual got the same level of care, and that was pretty neat to see. He AND his staff practiced what they preached.

It would take at least three books to explain the numerous political aspects in the medical community and between hospitals that Dr. Cowley had to work through. Suffice it to say that with his perseverance, and with the records of survival and recovery of critically injured patients, he was able to justify the fact that smaller hospitals could not provide the level of care necessary. However, convincing hospitals and emergency room staff to transfer patients that had arrived at their facility, or to reroute existing patients directly to the trauma unit, took a lot of time and effort. One of the key points, I believe, was the nursing workshops that were put together.

Four nurses from Shock Trauma were selected who had their own specialty areas; respiratory, psychiatric trauma, etc., and our traveling road-show was formed. We offered free training to the ER nurses at local hospitals and also brought many of them to the trauma unit to observe and participate in the care, and make them extended caregivers. Teaching nurses, it was very easy for the outlying hospital nurses to recognize their capabilities in comparison to those of the trauma unit nurses, and they as well began recommending to their doctors that certain patients could go to the trauma unit. With these nurse coordinators, we would do 2- and 3-day workshops at facilities all over the state, and we had a waiting list for classes. The nurses from Shock Trauma were all unmarried, young and attractive, so naturally my former compatriots in the ambulance service drew conclusions about my relationships with them. I left them to their imaginations. While it boosted my ego, our relationships were strictly professional. I had the utmost respect for those nurse coordinators.

Word spread. Other states asked Dr. Cowley for a MIEMSS/Shock Trauma symposium series. We started conducting them in 1972, which of course involved lots of travel to other states.

Not only did we provide the 'travelling roadshow,' we held tours and hosted internships. In fact, there was a waiting list of people from around the world who came to MIEMSS and the Shock Trauma Unit to observe and participate, and doctors and nurses who shared their expertise and experiences. It was not uncommon for us to have physicians from not only the military of the US, but from other countries as well, come and do an internship at the Shock Trauma Unit. A large number of these individuals initially were from England, and brought with them their native terminology, but it didn't take too long to understand that when they yelled for the 'lift' they were yelling for the elevator, and when they handed you your hat, they called it a 'lid.'

At the same time, the EMT program was spreading across the country. I spent less and less time at home, and more and more time being involved with EMT and CRT training.

The first class that we did at University Hospital was in the gray lab auditorium, where students sit in the rotunda-type area, and the instructor was in the middle of the place. Those of you that have seen the television program 'Doctor in the House' would recognize the shape of the facility. It was like a theater in the round to assist with the training of the students. We had a great cadre of instructors, and before long, physicians and nurses were scheduling themselves to give class lectures and share their expertise. This training was the DOT-approved EMT program of its day. Because of the facilities available, we expanded the program to include visits to the morgue for an autopsy of a cadaver, the burn unit and other specialty facilities.

At one time I had more jobs than I thought I would ever have, and often found myself going from the fire department ambulance, to the shock trauma unit, to the First Aid center at the Civic Center in downtown Baltimore to provide care for the circus, hockey games, wrestling, concerts, basketball games and other events. In addition, I was teaching one night a week in a community college in Frederick, MD.

The first helicopters Dr. Cowley arranged for to bring patients to the unit were military, and the initial heliport was outside the hospital in a square, bricked-in courtyard. We were always afraid somebody was gonna hit a wall landing.

Being only three blocks away, the ambo I worked on was the one that was routinely called when a helicopter came in, to pick up the patient and bring them to the unit. As soon as the hospital built a parking garage, the roof was designated as a landing zone for helicopters which was really nice, and much safer. However, when they built the parking garage, there were drainpipes that came down through the area where we had to drive the ambulance. Initially, we were riding in a boxy bus, a Schwab. In order for us to get up there, we could either go up the downramp and run into traffic coming out, or what we sometimes did - stop at the guard shack, and use their 3-step ladder to peel the bubble off the roof of the ambo so we fit through. Later, they put in the bell system so that when EMS arrived, a guard sounded the bell to alert everyone that an ambulance was on the ramp.

Later, the state police were brought in as Dr. Cowley worked his way through the politics. The police wanted helicopters, and the justification conveniently included not just police work, but patient transport as well. The first state helicopters were Bell Jet Rangers. We certainly wanted the flight medics to have at least the same training as the field people, so naturally MEIMSS developed the program and trained the MD State Police as EMTs/flight paramedics.

Over the years, Dr. Cowley worked very closely with the military, and they provided us with statistics and new technologies like advanced lab testing, CAT scanners, etc. before the rest of the world knew about them. However, the first big piece of specialty equipment that came to the Shock Trauma Unit was the hyperbaric chamber, which came from the Dixie Cup Company. It was located in the basement of the shock trauma area of the hospital, and in 1969 it was designated as a specialty referral center. To describe it, it was a gigantic cylinder you could walk in and operate, and it was divided into 3 sections. The center section was about the size of an elevator, and then on each end were treatment chambers and the pressures in those areas could be raised or lowered. So patients and staff would enter into the chamber, seal the doors and then the pressure would be elevated. This caused more oxygen to get into the blood system and keep body parts including the brain, heart and extremities alive due to the increased amount of oxygen that their circulation could transport. It was very good for smoke inhalation patients to flush the carbon monoxide out of the body, and also to enhance wound healing because of the increasing oxygen to the tissue. We gave familiarization tours to ambulance crews from around the state, usually in the evenings; they would have it as part of the EMT program. Looking back, one of the things we did down there was, it was pretty much a boring procedure for those on the outside. Close monitoring on all the people on the inside had to be maintained. As part of this, we had cameras in each of the sections that were displayed on TV screens, along with all the gauges and dials to operate the chamber. I would stand at the end of this, and all the students would be lined up looking at the gauges and stuff as we were talking about it. One of the operators decided to put a picture up in front of the camera, and it was an underwater picture similar to what you'd see in an aquarium. Then all of a sudden, a toy shark attached to a straw would be bounced across the picture. Now you've got the picture up there of the two chamber areas and then the entry area, so they were looking at two screens that were showing like just looking through the chamber, and then all of a sudden they'd see this shark bouncing across the screen, and I'd explain to them that, since they were building the harbor tunnel and the workers were subjected to the bends and pressurization and needed to be depressurized, we had a camera down there and were watching their operations. It was hard to hold my smile and there were usually a couple of nurses around too. And soon some of the nurses would come down and make busy work so they could watch the reactions of the students when they saw the shark on the screen and pointed to it, and everyone else started looking all around.

So the Shock Trauma Unit opened in the 1960s with 2 beds, and in 1973 a new building was built with 24 beds. That's when Governor Mandell created the Division of EMS under the MD Department of Health & Mental Hygiene, and also the MD Institute of Emergency Medicine (MIEM) in the University of MD (formerly the Center for the Study of Trauma).

Naturally, state resources were consolidated. Before 1975, the Emergency Medical Resources Center at Sinai Hospital had the first state-funded telemetry system, the Emergency Medical Communication System. I happened to be at Sinai, taking CRT instructor training, when an un-named doctor came in and announced, "That SOB just took everything." That was when MIEMSS began hosting the new state-operated facility, called SYSCOM. SYSCOM coordinated all med-evac transports by the MD State Police, US Park Police, US Army and the US Coast Guard.

Once Dr. Cowley had broken his ankle and was in a local hospital. Upon his discharge I picked him up to bring him back to the trauma unit, about 10 or 12 blocks away. As it was early in the morning, traffic was heavy. He was sitting on the stretcher, while we inched down one of the main thoroughfares. Dr. Cowley hollered, "What the hell are you doing? Turn on the lights and siren and get me down there!" I told him it would be inappropriate for me to run lights and siren, only to have the hospital staff that was waiting to pick him up from my vehicle see us running lights and siren even though he was stabilized, and I told him he was just being grumpy. He told me that he was the boss, and that I should do what he told me, and I told him that if I did, by the next day he'd be ripping me a new one. He'd have to explain to every-body, because I was not gonna take responsibility. Eventually, he told me I didn't know who the boss was, but we did proceed without lights and siren.

There came a time when Dr. Cowley began planning for someone to take over his position. He supported a certain doctor, but other doctors wanted to discredit Dr. Cowley so his support of this doctor wouldn't result in that doctor being selected. Three of those doctors wrote a letter of non-support/no faith to the hospital. A copy of the signed letter was made available to the press. A mysterious man did an interview from a restaurant not far from Lou's house, sitting behind a screen and using a voice-changer. Shortly after, objections to Dr. Cowley's recommendation were dropped.

TRAINING & COUNCILS

While I was still an ambulance attendant, word spread that there were gonna be changes in the training of ambulance personnel, and a number of individuals were selected nationally to go to Delaware and be trained as instructors under one of the original authors of emergency care, Harvey Grant. In my instance, I knew that the training was to take place but when I applied to my department, I was told that the selection had already been made by the deputy chief. I asked him if I had been considered, and he made it quite clear that the department head, for political reasons, had chosen select individuals to attend the training. I contacted Mr. Grant personally and explained to him that I was interested in being a part of the program, yet had been rejected by my department. He told me he had a pencil in his hand and he was writing my name on the list. If I could get there for the training, he would make me eligible. I went to my chief and put in for vacation for that timeframe, much to his dismay. My request was denied. I ended up going to the chief of the department and the board of commissioners, asking them to justify my not being able to utilize my own time for the training. The battalion chief relented and I was fortunate enough to attend that school, get the training, and come back to Maryland. As one of the original 116 instructors, we went out and trained other ambulance personnel in the standardized Department of Transportation (DOT) training. This was in 1972. At the same time, I still had my job on the ambulance. Over time, I became an instructor, evaluator and member of the Maryland Instructor Certification Review Board.

As training occurred and evolved, we were put under the auspices of the state Department of Health, and went out and had far-reaching programs in many areas of the state. All of the training equipment was standardized and kept in a central location, and we would pack up and go out and do the training, and at the conclusion of the training have written and practical exams to check the achievements of the students.

Efforts were made to improve the DOT, and the federal government put some money into the development of a better training program which turned into being the EMT training program. It started out at 81 hours of training. We always felt this was a little bit strange, in that in our state of Maryland it took over 1,000 hours to get a degree or to get a certificate to cut hair, yet 81 hours of training was sufficient to put someone's life in your hands. (As a benchmark to show how easy MD's EMT test was, we administered it to someone who had no medical training – my wife. A passing grade was 70. She scored 85.)

The training was met by major opposition in that, for the most part, those providing ambulance service felt they were doing a good job and wanted more money. So, like it or not, what it became was dollars and cents. The federal government not only developed the EMT program and supported it nationally in those states that adopted it, but they put financial backing into it and later on, grant monies for equipment and so on. So, the development did take place, although it was quite slow.

As an instructor, I gathered some unusual training aids. It wasn't uncommon to open up the freezer and find placentas in Tupperware bowls and stuff like that in there. My wife was not impressed, but my daughter once took a preserved heart to school for show-and-tell.

I spent many hours driving to the far reaches of the state and beyond, to teach classes on childbirth, CPR, rescue/extrication, and other topics. We also taught many different groups besides emergency responders and military, like first aid classes for the Boy Scouts and church groups. And we held training at many different locations. If we had to make room at a station house by pulling out the engines and conducting the training in the engine bay, we did it. We held auto extrication training at many different as junkyards, and even held training on the grounds of the DuPont Mansion in Delaware.

"OUR GANG"

In the beginning, we developed training materials on our own, staging and filming videos and snapping still photos, most often right at my house or in my yard. My two younger children were filmed climbing on top of the stove, and in other perilous scenes to demonstrate what NOT to do. My two older children were also involved in auto extrication training.

Once we were doing a training film on medevac protocols. As victims, we had an adult gentleman and my son, who was 15 or 16. For authenticity, we used real, outdated blood poured on their bandages. (Nothing looks like blood, like real blood does!) They were tied to backboards and we were filming, when we got a call for a real emergency. We all took off and left them there, for I guess quite a while. When we returned, we found that the man's wife had made no attempt to release them, and they were almost eaten alive by mosquitos!

We had, as with any new movement, people that were very enthused and some that were not. One instance that I remember was where we went to the far reaches of our state, did the training program and tested the students. The following day, we were told there would be a large meeting that evening, and it was required that we be there. At that point I was the Director for Pre-Hospital Care for the state of Maryland, and had to meet with this committee. As are most committees, this group was made up of experienced individuals that had many, many years working their way up the political ladders of the Volunteer Firemen's Association. To our dismay, a tirade started coming from some of the individuals as we sat down at the meeting. The immediate remarks that were made were complaining about testing, threatening to go to the press, and closing down the ambulance service for that area of the state, because they had taken and failed the test. They had been doing this for 40-something years, and they would go to the statehouse if necessary, and circle the statehouse with the ambulances due to this unfair situation and inappropriate testing. The individuals on the committee had probably not been on an ambulance for 20 or 30 years, but their rhetoric moved up the political, good old boy ladder within their communities. Our State Director at the time stated that he would look into it and get back to them. He looked at me and said, "This is unacceptable." I was concerned for the credibility of the program, and that the unfairness of the accusations would greatly impact our future training efforts.

During that time, the practical exams were given and the results of the practical exams were established at the time of testing. The written exams were given, and the answer sheets were brought back to the central office to be graded. After the meeting, I explained to the Director that the written exams that these individuals claim to have failed, had not even reached Baltimore to be graded, but were still coming up from the far reaches of the state. They had yet to be graded, and they had the impression, without even waiting to see what their grades actually were, that they had failed their exams. Their passing scores turned out to be similar to the scores of all others in other areas of the state; they hadn't done any worse or any better. Their scores fell right in the curve. It was impressive to see the state representatives immediately accept the allegation that the students had been wronged, even though their grades were hidden. (More on this topic can be found in the chapter *The Maryland Way*.)

We developed and initially taught the training program for the MD State Police, and then the US Park Police medevac helicopter programs. While the Maryland State police were operating their medevac, the US Park police in Washington, DC also had helicopters and requested training. We had staff members from both agencies in the same classes. As US Park police began flying patients, they were much closer to MedSTAR at the Washington Hospital Center and began to bring patients in there. This situation put me in the middle, as classes were made up of individuals from both organizations. Usually the students would come to the Shock Trauma Unit for their training in uniform and in their department vehicles. Some questioned why we were training our 'competition.' We were informed in the middle of a training session that we would no longer be training the US Park Police. The easiest solution from my perspective was to have the students come in as students, in civilian clothes, and park their vehicles off-campus. We didn't have competition in our minds, and we were able to continue training and finish the class. Later, MedSTAR and the US Park police developed a similar training program. One of the lead physicians that had helped form the Baltimore Shock Trauma Unit took over the MedSTAR receiving facility. This became a political 'helicopter wars.' While for most of our people, getting into the most appropriate facility was still the focus, it became a concern of losing patients or competing for patients. This did not trickle down in the efforts of the state police or US Park police medical operations, as the field providers just wanted to do the best they could for the patients.

In addition to developing and conducting training, I also spent a fair amount of time promoting health and safety, and speaking to groups all over Maryland to familiarize them with the state emergency medical system. My first TV appearance, I shared winter survival tips for motorists during cold weather – things like taping a dime to a jug.

We took every opportunity we could to demonstrate and teach. At one of the annual MD State Firemen's Association Conventions held in Ocean City, MD, I dangled from a MD state police helicopter over the water, demonstrating a water rescue.

New events and activities were always being organized. In Towson, MD in 1976, the first Annual Statewide EMS Olympics were held. At the Shock Trauma Unit, we had East vs West contests.

From 1976-1985, I was the Triage Office Go-Team Coordinator and prepared and carried out mass casualty exercises, furthering the concept of getting a doctor out to the field, on location.

In 1976 I was also involved in coordinating the first Disaster Drill at Baltimore's Inner Harbor during Preakness Week. Baltimore was hosting the USA Bicentennial EMS & Traumatology Conference, and we staged an underwater explosion, blowing up a ship in the harbor. Dr. Cowley watched the whole exercise from the bridge of a floating restaurant. Counties from across Maryland participated.

At another Disaster Drill, held at BWI Airport, we made use of satellite telemetry with Brooke Army Hospital in San Antonio, TX. It was the first time that satellite telemetry was used other than for military purposes.

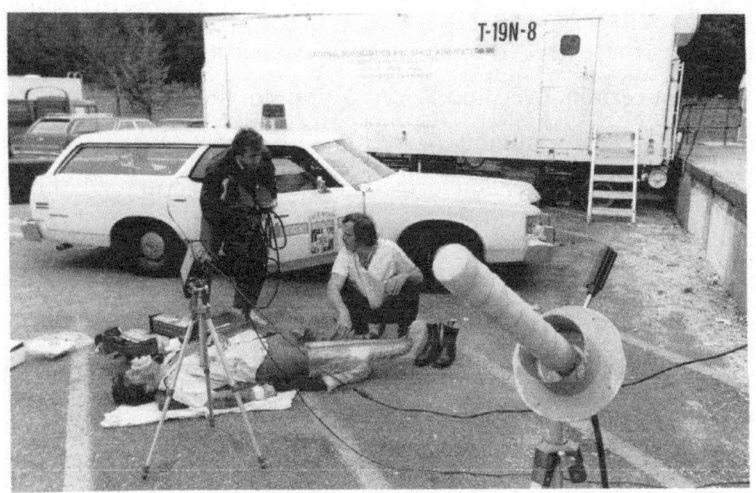

In order to use new technology like telemetry from an ambulance to a hospital, a CRT program was developed. This involved sending EKGs to a hospital and receiving medical direction on when and how to administer basic drugs or solutions. Other states were developing their own brands of CRTs, their own but similar programs. With the addition of more drugs and skills, the title eventually evolved into what would today be known as EMT-intermediate.

In 1982, I was an EMT Training Consultant to the US Department of Justice, and a group of us from MIEMSS traveled to Heidelberg, Germany to train US military personnel from all over Europe, in ACLS and ATLS.

Living near Martin State Airport, I often met flights coming in with organs or donor bodies, and transported them to local transplant centers. One time, I had my son and his friend with me for the transport of a donor heart/lung. When we arrived at the hospital, the doctors allowed them to watch the transplant 'in theater,' and later sent them both letters/certificates thanking them for their assistance.

I also joined several councils. I became a charter member of the National Registry of EMTs, and served as Regional Coordinator and member of the Practical Exams Committee. The National Registry of EMTs was founded after the government, DOT and other agencies were looking to standardize the training. There needed to be a way of evaluating and recognizing the training to a certain level, and Rocco Morando, founder of the National Registry, along with a number of well-qualified, well-recognized medical individuals, came together and formed the National Registry of EMTs. They developed a testing process and practical exam that could be administered across state lines and addressed the standardization of training and the level of practice in many areas. The level of practice was varied, as each state had their own ideas on what their state needed or could afford to do, and so there was difficulty. However, a number of states also thought that if you were able to be a soldier in Utah, you ought to be able to be a soldier in New Mexico. Teams of individuals often worked across state lines or local jurisdictions. We started out with everybody doing their own thing, doing what they thought was best, but not working collectively to see that we were indeed as good as our counterparts across the county, city or state lines. DOT generally was the one that specified what the minimal equipment would be.

The way the National Registry developed further was by putting together numerous committees and groups, including physicians and medical directors, to establish how we would train and test individuals to the national standard which was reflected by the National Registry of EMTs. The registry is a certification or recognition or measurement tool that individual states could apply to and be tested to. This was intended to do away with situations where EMTs were being trained to the standards of the local instructor, as those varied greatly. You could often tell by observing new students who had trained them, as they were like mirror images. The registry encountered much opposition, because it had the potential, in the eyes of the State Directors, of taking away their ability to make these national determinations. So we saw specific states or areas of a state determine they were going to write their own standards. But there was strength in saying, "We're as good as anyone else; we meet the national standards." This system continued to stand up to opposition by those who were, in my opinion, afraid of change or not receptive to change, and this may have been due to financial matters but, nonetheless, it was not an easy road for the Registry to be accepted by these states. But numerous organizations formed in specific states and specific areas, and they began to say, "We're as good as the next state over," and it became very interesting. But to show you an example, in one tri-state area that took in PA, WV and MD, we would have classes that had students from all 3 political subdivisions. They'd have the same training, and the same instructors, and would take the same examination. What concerned me at that time as the State Training Coordinator, was the students from one state were deemed qualified to practice for a certain period of time, say 2 years, before recertifying, and the students from another state were deemed qualified for 3 years before they had to recertify.

For a time, I was Chair of the Committee on EMS of the American Society for Testing and Materials (ASTM), where we worked on the first ASTM EMS national standard. In 1984 I worked with the group again as task group leader for ASTM F-30-02-02. Testing and materials were outside of government. Due to the number of states not adhering to DOT standards, an attempt was made to use ASTM to set ongoing standards. After a time, interest and participation faded away. But we did get ASTM to change EMT-A (Ambo) to accept EMT-B (Basic), so non-ambulance-based programs that didn't transport patients were able to give EMT-level care without being required to run in conjunction with ambulance services, i.e., ski patrol. This made EMT-trained people more available to the general public.

I spent 20 years on the National Council of State EMS Training Coordinators (NCSEMSTC), representing MD, USVI, Guam and the Northern Mariana Islands. The history of that council is something that I believe has been lost in historical references to the development of EMS in numerous areas. Initially, the DOT issued the EMT training program and as a result, most states assigned and identified an individual to be responsible for developing training programs for the advancement of EMS as time went by. The group that was formed was called the National Council of State EMS Training Coordinators. As EMS started, most of these positions were filled by senior instructors from within the states, and then as state agencies developed EMS councils and groups, these people were the ones that moved on and were responsible for designing and implementing EMT programs within their states. It was seen that we had many, many common areas that we were trying to address, and rather than just within our states, this gave us the opportunity to realize where we were with levels of training, and where we should consider going with levels of training.

Around the same time that there was a drive to move away from the federal government into the ASTM programs for future development, there was a gathering of state EMS training coordinators who had an annual conference and developed a great comradeship among states, sharing how to implement newer training programs, developing training outlines, and a number of these people were also utilized by the DOT which awarded some small grants to allow them to be a motivating force for continued training. Meetings were held specifically in areas away from large venues such as Disneyland and Las Vegas. They were held in out-of-the-way places where true concentration could be given to the tasks at hand.

One example of many was the development of the EMT defibrilator program. DOT awarded NCSEMSTC, as a group, the funding to develop a training program to train individuals to use defibrilators in the field. It was very interesting, in that a number of the states had been looking at this, but by coming together in a conference we could develop a program that would meet most needs and prevent states from going in different directions. This was another area that upset state directors.

Now this may seem like sour grapes but this is my perception of the national council as I participated for approximately 20 years. The sharing of this information apparently interfered with the ideas and vision of some the state directors who were coming into their own power, either being elected or designated as state leaders. The majority of them worked together, but it became quite obvious that there was apprehension in having their employees making recommendations to the DOT and showing unity of direction. Friction became obvious over the years, and the NCSEMSTCs for the most part ceased to exist as a National Council, as it was melded into the National Leaders Council. That's the way I see it, as it became obvious that the time was coming that the state directors would put a thumb down on the National Council's participation on national matters and in dealing with DOT.

One of the striking points that I wish to make is that fortunately, a history of the National Council and its activities was kept, and on numerous occasions we would collectively come up with a non-binding but a suggested step forward, such as a recommendation for extra hours of training, implementation of the esophogeal obturator airway (EOA), mast trousers, and other items and directions. I'm able to, and will present to any readers, a place where they can go back and read each of these documents that we issued. They were made in good faith for the government, at the state and federal levels. We had an actual working force of people that knew EMS training, and were willing to give and take to develop national standards. I'm sure that some of these will be quite eye opening when you look at the dates, and some of the old-timers will recognize the names of the individuals that signed for their specific states. This was us, as individual training coordinators, signing in a non-binding situation; these were our recommendations. However, the recommendations could have led the state directors to the belief that the organization was getting too big for its britches. The DOT recognized the value of the National Council, as well as a number of publishers coming to the National Council and saying, "You are the wealth of information, we wish to do this, could you review this textbook, piece of equipment" and so on. It made the leaders of the states a little bit shaky at times. But this is the true history of these documents. The reason I mention this is, as I said, not sour grapes, but I do not believe that the true history of EMS and its development has been told, and here you will see the actual documents and suggestions that were put out by the members of the National Council. It was a great organization that developed a lot of the impetus for the improvement of EMS across the nation and across the world, and I feel that a lot of that information has been ignored as we indoctrinate our new EMS people with the step-by-step we did this right, we did this right, we did this right—never mentioning that some of these ideas didn't work.

I believe that the National Council was one of the main branches, if not the trunk, of the EMS tree as it developed. I will leave it at that. While we had some very good relationships, there were also some empire builders that wanted everything done their way, and you never hear that story. You never hear that we made mistakes and so on. If so, as far as aviation you would probably be told that the Wright brothers invented an airplane, and 3 days later DC7s were flying around the world. They seem to have left a lot out of our history. So, take it for what it's worth and please go to the site and click on the individual documents and look at the suggestions and so on, and see how many of them are actual steps that were taken successfully to advance EMS. We had our share of failures as well as many great successes. But we had fewer failures because the National Council came together and recommended these changes.

In 1984, the annual conference took place in Austin, TX, and we all attended a local rodeo. Several other training coordinators rode, receiving various injuries, but that didn't stop me from following suit. I was given the Jackass of the Conference Award by fellow members, and came home in a wheelchair.

Who can count the number of conferences and trade shows that Lou attended and presented at over the years? Among all the EMS legends he met, were a few personalities that even non-EMSers would know.

I first met Rod McKuen at Carnegie Hall when I was in town giving training with MIEMSS nurses. When he came to Baltimore, we went for a walk, and posed for a photo at the Edgar Allen Poe monument. On our walk, we found a kitten under a dumpster. He took it and named it Edgar, even though it was a female. He was responsible for turning me on to sheepdogs, and I had a few and raised them for several years.

I met Randolph Mantooth (who played John Gage on the TV show *Emergency!*) when he showed up at one of the firehouses, and saw him many times over the years at different conferences and trade shows.

THE MARYLAND WAY

T he MD Way was a skills manual to ensure that all trainees were trained and evaluated on their skills in the same exact manner. It started when Dr. Cowley was informed by the state EMS group that they had been informed that their students were unable to pass the practical exam and were threatening to protest by circling the state house and by threatening to close down ambulance services. The way this happened was amazing, as it came from out of the blue and hit us in a statewide meeting. The state was divided into 5 regions and each region had a regional council. Most of the people on these regional councils were experienced EMS providers, but a large portion were not. The groups were made up of those with political clout in each region. Our EMT testing process was that students would be trained, and upon signature of completion of the training program, evaluations or practical exams would be scheduled. Generally, classes were tested individually, although there were occasions where due to the number of students it was more effective to have larger evaluation processes, and have students from numerous classes tested at the same time and location.

EMT instructors had instructor manuals and lesson plans that were all the same. However, most instructors wanted to do a better job, or feeling that they knew better than what the national program was teaching, started to develop their own special ways of providing practical skills. This created major problems when we tested a group, especially a mixed group such as those by two different instructors taught on two different locations, and brought together for the practical examination. The evaluators of the practical stations were given sheets with the activities to be recorded, and the scores for each activity were added up, leading to a pass or fail of that particular skill. An easy way to explain this would be, if the goal was to immobilize a fractured radius. The end result was to be that the bone was aligned, immobilized with a splint, and held to the body with a sling and swath. Some instructors felt it wasn't necessary to use a board splint; others felt they could accomplish the end goal of immobilization with only a sling and swath; others felt that the board had to extend beyond the fingertips of the individual; while others felt that the board splint should be dressed with the fingers over the end of the board and immobilized in that position, maintaining the hand and wrist in a position of function. Evaluators, who were all instructors and trained as evaluators for practical skills, all seemed to either accept the step-by-step procedures, or to develop their own procedures which varied from the standard testing. Many times, variables were not failure points, but indeed were variables in the steps taken. And there were some steps that need not be taken, but did not constitute the students' inability to accomplish the end result. These were instructor preferences, and as we all know, every instructor had a better way or their way of accomplishing the end result. What led to the major problems and the need for the development of The MD Way was when a special state meeting was called and the representatives of the 5 regions were in attendance. However, they had already made their threats to withdraw from the state program via phone with Dr. Cowley prior to the meeting.

Testing had been done in one specific region, we'll say on a Monday evening. Students, assuming that they had failed, went to their regional representatives and complained. Their representatives set up a meeting with Dr. Cowley to discuss this inappropriate testing, and they made the statement time and again that their students were failing and were going to withdraw from providing ambulance service in their specific area. The amazing part of all this was, that the students who were tested on Monday, their papers were not yet recorded or evaluated, but were put in an envelope containing both the written examination questions and the practical exam sheets, and were all brought to the central office in Baltimore and graded a few days following.

This assured that all the exams had the same answer keys. It was automated to the point that all answers regardless of what region the test had been administered in, etc. was subjected to the same gradient level. The complaints at the statewide meeting from one area of the state, was that they took the test, and they just "knew" that they failed it, and therefore they were going to quit providing service. The most interesting fact was that their test had not even been graded and had just arrived in Baltimore hours before this command meeting was started. The fact that these students were so adamant that they had been unfairly treated set off a firestorm. Our explanation from the state office that the exams had not even been graded at this point fell on deaf ears. It didn't matter whether they did or didn't fail, they "felt" they had failed and therefore created major uproar in the testing process. When that was explained at the public meeting, and the validity of the testing process was questioned, after lengthy discussions Dr. Cowley decided that the instructors should not be putting in their own variables as a replacement to the standard testing procedures. These were the practical skills being addressed. We made it clear that the same written examination and the same practical examination was being given, administered to students in some instances from Pennsylvania, West Virginia and Maryland. Yet these outbursts of lack of faith and lack of facts continued to concern the state officials, and the mandate was to develop or redevelop the testing forms that allowed one way to perform a practical skill and, as Dr. Cowley quoted, there will be one way to do something, the students will be trained to do it that way, and tested to do it that way, and that way will be the way we approve. There will be no variance in the practical skills exam process. I mentioned to the attendees that it was difficult to explain why none of the other regions or students from neighboring states had these problems. The facts and figures were there. The problem was that the instructors and evaluators were deviating from the guidelines. It was also interesting that graduates from the same training program that were on border states, that had attended the program in Maryland and were tested under those same procedures at the same time and location, had much higher passing grades than the Maryland students, where evaluators were teaching their own brand of skills. That fell on deaf ears. I also questioned that in one state where an exam was held and students from multiple jurisdictions or states were tested and evaluated using these consolidated exams, how could it be that those that passed from one state would be certified for 2 years, and yet another state may have a 3- or 4-year certification based on them passing the same exact test at the same exact location. I openly asked the group, "Is it true that there is a mentality barrier where the students from one state only get ½ the certification timeframe and others get more?" This as well fell on deaf ears.

At the conclusion of this meeting, Dr. Cowley made it clear that as the Director of EMS for the state of Maryland, he would approve the skills and how they would be performed for all Maryland classes. He stated there would be one way, and that would be his way, the Dr. Cowley way. He mandated us to develop a clear, concise step-by-step evaluation form that would be utilized state-wide from that point forward, and that we do it "immediately or sooner."

As word of this concern spread, which was very quickly, the majority of Maryland instructors felt they knew the best way to do it or an alternative way to do the skills. Hearing and fearing that instructors would be unable to teach alternate or additional steps and skills, an outcry arose from the instructors and evaluators. In order to start on the implementation of a one-way skills evaluation document, I set a meeting for each of the 5 regions, inviting the instructors and evaluators, and we went out to explain what had happened and why. At a number of these meetings the instructors and evaluators rejected the thought that there was one way of doing something and that they would be restricted from teaching their way or an alternate way. The meetings got quite heated and tempers flared. The next step was to develop this alternate 'MD Way' of evaluating skills and presenting it to the instructors in a second series of meetings. In order to provide them a starting point, we gathered 8 instructors and our audio-visual team from the state EMS office. We videotaped each skill being done by one instructor using the state form that was in the process of being developed as the standardized new MD Way skill. We then returned to the regional office meetings with the instructors and evaluators, and showed them what skill would be taught, what way, and evaluated what way. Those were probably some of the roughest meetings I had in my career with the evaluators and the instructors. Remarks were made such as the people that are complaining, don't know what they're complaining about, some of them haven't been on an ambulance for 30 years, etc. etc. And the fact was, that the complaining region, when their exams were graded after the first meeting, found that they had no worse fail rate than any of the other regions, but that didn't matter to them. We had been instructed to develop one way of doing each skill and put it in a skills manual. The instructors and evaluators were in an uproar and some threatened to quit teaching and to continue the battle. I suggested that we had as a group, 3 options. You could quit teaching, and leave the students with lesser classes and lesser potential of becoming EMTs; you could sit back, keep your mouth closed and accept whatever the state presented; or you could join together and become a part of the development of The MD Way, knowing full well you may not get your specific variance included, but with all of us working together we could buy some time and develop one skill that was acceptable or semi-acceptable to most all instructors. I pointed out to them that they were the strength of the training program, and it was up to them to show their dedication to the program and to help us develop it. It seemed as if that worked and the majority of them wanted to be a part of the development. There were some nasty remarks made at these meetings, such as incompetent, over-the-hill, people speaking for the EMTs, etc. etc. It was not my job to defend the regional councils, but to develop the single skills evaluation for training and testing. I certainly knew we could do it much better with the input of all the instructors. We filmed one way of doing each skill and we filmed it on the front lawn of a home, no studio, no major script, just the hands-on, eyes-on video of what was to be expected with the new MD Way. We lost very few evaluators or instructors as most of them joined in, supporting us with the development. As we began to finalize the skills, another statewide meeting was called and prior to that meeting, Dr. Cowley called and told me to get over there early, and to get something to eat because it was going to be a long night. He didn't say why or what was going on, but it was obvious that he was expecting problems, and it also appeared to me that I had the target on me at this meeting. In the meeting, individuals from some regions reported to Dr. Cowley that I had conducted meetings where their credibility had been questioned, that they were called out-of-touch, incompetent, old farts that knew nothing about what they were complaining about. I looked at Dr. Cowley and he said, "Well?" I told him and the group that the individuals at these meetings, the instructors and evaluators, had indeed said these remarks and others that I wouldn't even repeat in the meeting. That they were all very well represented as an incompetent group that was uninformed and had reacted with no credibility to the remarks of the instructors and evaluators. I informed Dr. Cowley that for us to have the support would be much more advantageous to the successful development of the one-way skills training and evaluation, than for 2 or 3 people to develop it and cram it down the throats of the instructors and evaluators. They were given three choices: quit instructing and give up everything they had worked for; roll over and accept whatever a small group came up with; or join together and help me and the MIEMSS staff develop an acceptable manual of skills for teaching and evaluation. The room was pretty much deadly quiet until one individual who just happened to be the Director of the MD Fire and Rescue Institute spoke up and said, "Hold it a minute." He said, "I had my staff at each and every one of these meetings," and he said, "My people reported to me and I'm going to state to you that what we had here was, that Lou went into the regional meetings and had a lynch mob facing him and what he accomplished was, he gave them an alternative, and a viable alternative, and the lynch mob was turned into a posse" and that the majority of people wanted to participate in the development of The MD Way. He said, "The information the rest of you have put in here may have been factual with the remarks, but the results were that Lou turned this around, and that's the American way." That individual was John Hoglund and of the many people who were at the meeting, he carried more clout than any of the attendees, and was on par with Dr. Cowley. There was very little discussion after Mr. Hoglund's clear and accurate reflection of what had happened.

The meeting ended and as the guests all left, Dr. Cowley turned to me and my MIEMSS partner at the time, and said, "I won't need to talk to you." He had previously told us to come early, get a meal and be prepared for a long night, yet at the conclusion of the meeting he said there would be no need to go on with any further discussion. At that point I challenged his decision to cancel us discussing the matter, and asked him if we could not meet right then. He nodded his head and we went into his office. I told him that I was very concerned that he had heard and listened to the unjustified complaints from a number of the regional representatives and yet had not discussed it with me prior to the meeting. I told him I felt he owed me more than that. He looked at me, smiled and ended the conversation with, "There will be one way, and you and your team will develop it, and it'll be my way," and I said, "Yes, sir." He responded with, "If I had been at those meetings, I would have been eaten alive. So write the damned thing. Now let's go to Burke's for hamburgers and onion rings." We never discussed that night again.

That ended the turmoil over The MD Way. It took us months, we had meetings statewide to allow for input, and The MD Way was developed. As the book was developed and prepared for printing, one of the MIEMSS administrators who had no input into the development of the book wanted the credit for the book, for The MD Way Manual. As I had had frequent differences of opinions and direction from this individual, I told the publishers of the book that I wished to not have my name associated with the book, even though I had been the Project Director. Probably a childish response on my part, but it made it clear that I felt that those who put in the work developing it deserved credit; not just a political empire builder.

ISLANDS

The story of my involvement with the US Virgin Islands (USVI) began with a phone call from the Director of the EMS there, Kirk Grabowski. Kirk was one of the most influential and interesting people I met in my life. He and his wife had settled in the Virgin Islands and raised their family there by choice, not because they were 'Born There.'

I mention this because there was, and is, clearly a distinction made as to one's stature and acceptance of individuals based upon their place of birth. Unfortunately, this is seen quite clearly in government, as nepotism runs rampant. Outsiders or those born elsewhere are, in many instances, not afforded the same opportunities as those who by a quirk of fate are 'Born Here' Islanders.

This is not unlike the discrimination we see between Yankees and Southerners here in the eastern United States. It is a fact of nature that people are more comfortable and naturally gravitate to forming societies of 'like people.' However, with a smaller population and close family ties, it is easy to see how an island nation would be prone to favoring 'like people.' A large portion of the citizens share the same family tree. Family relationships often take precedence when job opportunities are available, and such a system does not assure that the right person gets the right position.

Kirk was un-phased by the system, and in spite of the hurdle and obstacles such a system had, he found a way to be accepted on the basis of his efforts and perseverance.

With the development of the EMT programs nationally in the US, came grant monies and incentives to assist in developing state and local programs. Hearing of this, Kirk found that the USVI would be eligible for help. He applied and was awarded an initial grant.

In 1976 I was visited by Kirk, a tall, lanky individual wearing a flowered shirt, shorts and sandals. He had some of the biggest feet I had ever seen. These proved to be well worthwhile, as he needed them for a firm foundation to stand up to all of the political BS he would deal with throughout the years. He had recently been appointed by the government of the USVI to oversee the new program called Emergency Medical Services. It's interesting that Kirk had his initial degree in environmental studies, and went to the islands to help them with their refuse problems. Being as politically incorrect as one could be, Kirk ruffled some feathers and following usual government solutions, he was assigned duties in a different field, EMS. He showed up in my office and asked if there was a potential of assisting them with their EMS program as they moved through the fledgling steps. There was no doubt in my or his mind, that the drive was not only to create an EMS program, but also to qualify for some federal grant money, as their program, as I was to find out, was in a shambles. I went to Dr. Cowley with Kirk. Kirk quickly explained he would like any assistance we could give him, and Dr. Cowley said it sounded like a fine idea and for me to take care of it. Dr. Cowley's 'take care of it' response was one I heard many times throughout the years. I am pleased that he gave me so much leeway to get things done, and as long as I reported progress back to him, he said, "good deal" and turned me loose again. So, I had quite a bit of latitude based on my relationship with Dr. Cowley.

I became the EMS training consultant for the USVI, and over time a meeting was arranged with the Governor, and I flew down. Shortly thereafter I was escorted into the Governor's office by two six-foot-something bodyguards. I was quite impressed with the Governor (government king) who had brilliant white hair, a strong-looking individual who obviously had full control over everything in the Islands. One of the things that I found out quickly, was that everybody was related to everyone else, and it was not uncommon when the Governor left the Island to go to a meeting, that the Lieutenant Governor would bring in all of his family members and the others would start drawing unemployment, only to change when the Governor returned. It was like having two part-time governments. But it did give us the opportunity to deal with lots of people, and on occasion we would wait until one person was off Island and deal with the other. The politics were not unlike many of us have used in going to the person that you thought would give you the answer you were looking for.

The first step was when Kirk took me to the hospital and started introducing me to the ambulance drivers and emergency room staff, the Commissioner of Health and the Director of Nursing. It was easy to recognize that they indeed needed some guidance, as the vehicles they were driving had doors that were either taped shut or held together with belts, were banged up and had minimal equipment available. In talking with the ambulance drivers, it became quite evident that most of them were taxicab drivers. Not the type that some consider our ambulance services being taxis, but these were real 'make a living off the tourists' taxicab drivers. The required education was minimal at that time, and we were pleased to find that some of them did have basic first aid training. However, they had no equipment to practice it with.

There was one hospital on St. Thomas, and two on St. Croix which was a larger island, and a clinic on St. John which was a smaller nearby resort island. Working with Kirk and the federal EMS governmental personnel, Kirk was able to get a grant for equipment and we started making plans and preparing the ambulance drivers for change.

Most were not pleased and were more concerned that if they failed some of the training, they would lose their part-time jobs. We held a meeting and explained to them that the goal was not to replace anyone, but to work together as a team and upgrade both their equipment and their capabilities.

We won them over. Shortly thereafter, ambulances from the continental US arrived at the government holding station motor pool. We waited weeks and weeks for them to approve these new, shiny vehicles and only got them released to the Department of Health after calling to the attention of the Governor that the motor pool personnel were driving them around the Island, yet none had been released to the hospitals or EMS service. A phone call from the Governor changed that, and the ambulances showed up quickly.

The ambulances they had been using were converted vans with a red light on the top, and a radio system that had less capabilities than most of us had in our own cars with CB radios. The Islands also are the tips of mountains, so with the hills and so on, there were many dead areas. As far as equipment, they had Band-Aids, some curlex, a couple of boards, a stretcher and usually an oxygen tank rolling around in the back of the ambulance which I never saw used.

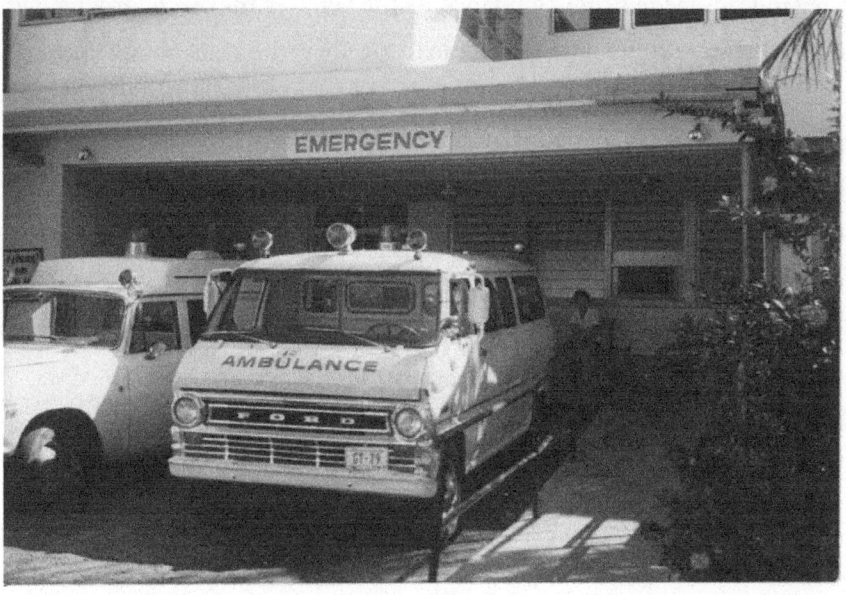

In the beginning, as they were stationed at the hospital, all the drivers had for duties were to see that the ambulances were fueled and relatively clean, and to make sure the doors stayed closed and were secured. Quite frankly it was a very sad state of affairs.

I think it's important to mention a few of the points that were of great concern to me, that definitely kept the level of care in the hospital at a low level. While these have been corrected long ago, just imagine what it would be like to have an emergency room and if an EKG were needed for a patient, the nursing staff or physician would have to contact the one EKG technician at home, and send an ambulance to pick them up and bring them in to the hospital. And not because others couldn't run the machine, but because the EKG technician was protecting her job and was paid to come in to do the EKG. In addition to that, the head nurse, due to a shortage or theft of drugs, would often bring the painkillers home with her, and likewise had to be contacted to come in with the drugs. Ambulance drivers going on calls were also expected to pick up ice for the hospital. Laundry etc. were other functions that over time were addressed and handled as well. As time went by and grant monies were made available, we found more and more advances in the level of care being made.

One of the other points that we think made an impact, was the nursing staff had only used the ambulance people to bring a patient in and then they sat outside awaiting the next call. Calls were few and far between, and most of them were made up of half-Islanders with the usual injuries and illnesses. And then a different community – that being the tourists from cruise ships that either phoned or came in. Tourists would come off the ship into the hot and humid Island climate. Most of them were 30 years or older, and coming off the air-conditioned ship into the humid Caribbean climate, it was not uncommon to receive a number of calls for heat-related conditions. So, there were actually two sets of potential patients that they would deal with.

The nursing staff was concerned when they heard that one of the promises made to the EMTs was that they would undoubtedly be receiving consideration of a pay raise upon successful completion of the EMT training. The pay scales for nurses and EMTs was low for both occupations, and the nurses certainly didn't want to be left out.

I was surprised when we received the applications for the first class, to see that a number of nurses, both LPNs and RNs, had applied. For the most part, the nurses didn't realize how happy I was to have them in the class, as they had skills that we were able to utilize, sharing these skills with the ambulance attendants. Initially there was no exchange of information and very little care-giving outside of the hospital. Certainly the 'swoop and scoop' method that we laughingly referred to in the past was the norm. There was no such thing as an EMT and no state certification.

We had on occasion a need for interpreters for certain words and terminologies, and I think that one of the most important things that we did in the program was to really bend over backwards to assure that the students had the information that they needed. Virgin Islanders are made up of many individuals that have come from neighboring communities, neighboring islands, etc. So, a class may very well be a combination of those that had French as a first language, or Dutch as a first language and English as their second language. It was not unlike having to deal with a group at the United Nations on occasion. Most of the individuals, being proud, would not let you know they had questions. A number of students would nod their head in agreement that they understood something, but the instructors were not sure they really did.

The instructors for the first class were predominately individuals from within that community, and a couple State of Maryland EMS instructors that came down. It wasn't difficult to find good instructors that I personally knew, so a number of different instructors had the opportunity to come down. We provided them housing and food and a plane ticket, and plenty of time to work with the students, and they all found time to build a vacation into the opportunity.

One of the things that motivated the students was the development of their own EMT patch, which we did during the confines of the training prior to anyone reaching the end. It kind of gave them a goal of being able to be recognized as someone special in the community, and they developed their own patch in the shape of a drop of blood emblazoned with palm trees in the sunset. It's still one of the prettiest patches that I have in my collection.

Finding a place to do the training was difficult. It was done at numerous locations – Health Department offices, the community college, and predominately especially on St. Thomas, at the old Red Cross building which was located right on the waterfront. Due to the humidity and closeness of the training room, we took frequent breaks and did all of our practical work in the outside alley. On occasion if the weather was bad or we had to get back to classroom training, we'd borrow a generator from the Civil Defense Agency and then run a cord from the generator, which we placed in the dumpster down the alley to muffle the sound, and had a cord running back into the classroom.

Newspaper people were down taking pictures, and the next thing you knew we were on the front page of the newspaper. And the general public got behind the idea of moving things ahead. That was a blessing in disguise because it wasn't uncommon for people to gather at the end of the alleyway and watch what we were doing. As everybody was related to everybody, we built support from the general public very quickly.

I made many friends, not only within the class but in the government, where representatives such as the Commissioner of Health and the Director of Nursing were very interested in making sure that the community knew that this was a great new capability that they were bringing to the Islands. So the support for the most part was very, very good. It was nice to see the LPNs coming into the EMT training program. They began to realize that important information could be brought in, and that the EMTs could take a blood pressure in the emergency room as well as reporting what they had on the scene, and that these were tools that made the nurses' jobs easier, and fostered teamwork.

This also led to the nurses going out on the ambulance and doing patient care in the field, as far as getting patient assessments, etc. and when the radios worked, even getting advance notification back to the emergency room.

I've told you enough of the negatives that we initially encountered, but I think that far more important is the drive of these individuals. How much many with only a grade-school education were able to achieve. They studied hard. Classes were from early morning until usually 3:00 or 3:30 in the afternoon, yet it was not uncommon for the class to remain half-filled until 5:30 or 6:00, with students tutoring other students, including the nurses and so on. We had a volunteer group of individuals that had teamed up to help each other to reach successful completion of the course.

I remember one individual that had originally come from Trinidad. He told me that his next-door neighbor had helped him learn to read and write. Well, he obviously didn't have a college education, and reading the EMT textbook was extremely difficult for him. We gave him a yellow magic marker and told him for his reading assignment, to go through the pages and highlight anything that he didn't clearly understand or that didn't make sense to him. It didn't take long to check his book as we were sitting there with him going over what was covered in class. It was basically all yellow pages, as he was really having a rough time understanding. However, during the classroom training, questioning him made it clear that most of the important points were clear to him, but that he would express them in a different way. Quite often when dealing with him, he would get up and get the overhead transparency and do a mini class for us so that we knew he was getting the concept. I'm sure that those of you who are instructors have had students that needed that little extra help to get over a hurdle. This is one of the students that I am proudest of, in that in the years following, he moved to New York and became a member of the New York Fire Department EMS network. From the kid that had a neighbor that tried to teach him to read, to a full-grown man who would not let this hurdle beat him, is indeed a great accomplishment.

We had numerous RNs and LPNs who started dropping in and signing up for the class. This was interesting in that there had been a complete wall of responsibility between those of the nurses and those of the EMTs. Remember at this time, ambulance attendants weren't even taking blood pressures or pulse rates on patients. It was truly a 'swoop and scoop' operation. The EMTs were not as concerned about the nurses coming in to the classes as some of the hospital staff was. They felt they were going to lose nursing staff to become EMT personnel. Of course, we found out very quickly that the whole thought process of the nurses was that they expected with a new healthcare classification, provider raises would be appropriate, and they were looking forward to advance their futures. Some of the EMTs were very nervous that they would be losing their jobs if they did not pass the EMT qualifications, so with these undercurrents going back-and-forth, we just moved forward with the training and let the chips fall where they did.

The classes were quite amazing in that, for example, we had to make adjustments. If we were to be using overhead transparencies or slides, we needed electricity to run the audiovisual devices. This was accomplished by borrowing a generator from the Civil Defense Unit, putting it in the alley in a dumpster, and running extension cords back from the alley into the classroom area, leaving the doors open for lighting inside, and using the grumbling generator to operate the overhead projector inside. I am certain that there were very few places that were being subjected to such harsh conditions in the rest of the free world, but at the same time I was able to recognize the dedication and devotion of the people that were in the class. Many of these people had very little and were not living the life of luxury, but were family people living as heads of households, and doing their jobs as best they could, being pretty ingenious working with what they had, like the tape and belts I mentioned earlier being used to hold the ambo doors closed.

We all worked very hard to bring along as many people as we could help and offer them extra training. We were fortunate to find a couple of nurses who had experience in the continental US. We also located a male nurse who was working as a crew member on a charter boat. He had been a paramedic in the service years before, and was working part-time as a nurse when they didn't have a cruise going on. He came on board as an assistant instructor and we had classes for extra-motivated students and so on, so we built our own cadre of instructors as time went on.

We had one student that sticks in my mind who lived in a tool shed in the Lagoon. The Lagoon was St. Thomas' nudist community, where there were boats that had been patched up and stripped of all valuable hardware, and were just floating bedrooms for the majority of the people. He not only lived and slept on a mattress in the tool shed, but we found as we moved to the rescue and extrication portions of training, that he didn't even have shoes or sandals to wear. So, we did a quick raid at the Red Cross disaster area and found him some shoes and long pants to wear, with a rope for a belt. I know this may sound funny or strange, but everybody pulled together to help each other. As we brought in equipment for different segments of the classes, it was clear that most of the equipment had never been seen there, raising great interest from Customs and the power and light company, as well as the fire department.

So we found people were signing up for other classes, and we truly ended up with a multi-organizational group where we could we use the skills of each of the people and their expertise, giving everyone a chance to share their knowledge, techniques and perspectives.

While I was there in the Islands, we had the opportunity to do training on all three Islands and trained not just the advanced people in nursing, but people that volunteered, such as librarians and people with the power and light company, a firefighter or two, and a number of general citizens. These people knew they would not qualify for an EMT job, as there weren't that many jobs available, but were very interested in helping each other. One of the problems I found with unions is they became too focused on income, and did not see the value of learning something unless they were going to get paid for it. While we had a couple of police officers and customs officers from the airport as a part of the class, there were those that were just looking for the opportunity to get a union position.

Remember we had no pre-screening for the students at that time, and this resulted, in my honest opinion, in varying levels of both motivation and capabilities. But the people of the Islands seem to have a special bond and work together to achieve. I saw some of the greatest teamwork accomplished by this makeshift group of individuals training, done at the police academy on St. Croix, and on St. John's at the Superintendent of the Parks' residence overlooking St. John's Bay and the sail and tour boats. But due to the low call volume, we needed to get experience and build morale and understanding in the students that had completed basic training. I was able to convince Mr. Grabowski (who took very little convincing), the Governor, the Commissioner of Health and the Director of Nursing that it would be worthwhile to their students to bring a few of them state-side in order to accomplish this. Funding was a major issue; however, the Islands were able to obtain courtesy airfare for transportation to Baltimore, and with the support of the Baltimore County, Baltimore City and Anne Arundel County ambulance services, and with Dr. Cowley's blessing, we brought the first group of 8 students to Maryland.

They stayed in my home, being picked up every morning by the appropriate ambulances for their day's duty. The neighbors were concerned the first morning, when a couple of the ambulances that arrived to pick up their students hit the siren rather than banging on the door. I got that cleared up after the first day. Each individual was given from the USVI $10 per day per-diem, so when I picked them up at the airport, our first stop would be the food store. They generally neglected to bring anything to eat; however, they never forgot bottles of rum and bags of curry powder for their West Indian food. The West Indian atmosphere of my home certainly surpassed my Italian grandmother's home for months. Each group only stayed a week. They came in on Tuesday, and then the following Tuesday morning I would drop them off at the airport, and wait to greet the next group.

While training in the USVI, I was pleased to obtain a device called a cardio beeper, which was one of the first basic telemetry type devices. It was made up of a 9-volt battery and a little box with two paddles that were placed on the patient. It then emitted an oscillating sound. The other half of the unit was a round ring attached to a similar box with three leads coming out of it. One evening while on St. Thomas, we realized that St. Croix had an EKG machine in its emergency room. We had no idea if it would work, so we tested it.

St. Croix was about 30 miles away, so it was transmitted over a microwave system to the phone in the St. Croix emergency room. By plugging the three electrodes into their EKG machine, and putting the circle ring around the earpiece of the telephone, we were able to transmit an EKG the 30-something miles over the 9-volt battery operated device. I believe that unit is currently in the National EMS Museum display.

On the occasion that we completed training on all three islands, the government allowed us to have EMS Day in the USVI, resulting in a large well-publicized gathering on St. Thomas with all the dignitaries in attendance.

Speaking to the most important guests were Rocco Morando, Director of the National Registry of EMTs, and his wife Theresa. This had been their first time to the Islands, and Rocco had worked very diligently with us and the government to ensure the integrity of the training program. He was well received, and in the years thereafter, never failed to mention what a great occasion that was. The Park Service provided Jeep-loads of coconuts, and food of all types, and a substantial amount of alcohol was consumed as we danced and made merry on the beach.

During this period of time, the Islands obtained a boat approximately 30 foot, named the Star of Life II. (The Star of Life I was stationed in Connecticut.) The owner of Fairfield Medical Products assisted us in obtaining a boat and outfitting it with all the necessary equipment found in an ambulance. That boat was stationed on St. John, which had a clinic rather than a hospital, and was utilized to transport patients to and from St. Thomas. Having the Star of Life II gave us the opportunity to include a good water rescue program. That is the first and last water rescue program that I took part in, in the USVI. While many of the Islanders were used to swimming in St. John's Bay, they had difficulty convincing me that a nurse shark would not bite. Having completed my training, I stayed on the deck with the captain and helped with the direction from a safe spot. I was on the Board of Directors for the Star of Life Flotilla in 1984, and the boat is still functioning today, being used for aircraft down in the water, missing divers and other emergency situations.

Considering that all of this started in 1976, more than 40 years ago, it is rewarding to know that this program continues to be in place and growing due to our involvement. I continue to have numerous friends and returned to the Islands as often as I could. Over the years we have continued our relationship with the USVI and attended numerous graduations and anniversaries of EMS milestones. Things are not perfect there, but they are far, far better than they would've been without the help of a lot of individuals.

Later, I was able to assist the Saint Maarten Emergency 24 Rescue Squad, and also worked with the Cayman Islands during their training, testing and evaluation, assuring that National Registry of EMTs standards were upheld. All three of these Caribbean locations required that the government of those territories accept in writing their intent to utilize the National Registry as their standard certification level.

On one occasion that I had the opportunity to spend some time with my two oldest children, I brought them down to the USVI with me. We landed at the airport. The ambulance was there, as well as some of the class members, and we climbed in and headed towards the world-famous Lagoon. As we were driving out, I asked my son who was approximately 8 years old, what he thought about the Islands. He said, "It's very pretty, and there's lots of flowers and goats running all over the place." Leaving downtown with the hotels and where the upper strata of the community lived, he began to notice the tin shacks with rusted metal roofing. I told him that we were going to an area where we would be seeing people who were so poor, they didn't even have clothes, which raised an eyebrow on my daughter who was 12. When we got to the Lagoon, we were welcomed by a large number of individuals of all ages and their families at Poor Man's Bar, which was the 'City Hall' of the Lagoon where everybody ate. A gentleman used his inflatable boat with a one-cylinder motor on the back to shuttle us from the bar to the houseboats. We went out to a houseboat called *Happy Days*, a 54-foot double deck boat that was sometimes used as a home for myself and two nurses while we did training there. As we approached the back of *Happy Days*, one of the nurses opened up the swim deck, stood forward and greeted us with, "Welcome to

Happy Days!" My daughter didn't seem to have any major concerns; if so, she didn't express them. However, my son looked up and saw her in nothing but her bare skin, and immediately put his head down to the point that his chin was about touching his chest. He was looking up through his eyebrows. He didn't make any remarks or anything other than a big grin. We got out of the boat, everybody exchanged hellos, and someone asked who wanted to cool off and have a swim. The boat was anchored in about 15 to 18 feet of crystal clear water, where you could see the bottom, with fish and a stingray floating around. It was indeed a beautiful place to be, and within 15 minutes everyone had removed their clothing and were swimming. My wife at the time had no idea that the Lagoon existed, but I swore the children to secrecy. For a period of time upon our return home, I never heard any questions or worry about it, so I don't know how long it was before they explained to their mother, but I never got anything out of her other than shaking her head and a smile. So evidently I hadn't corrupted them.

The Lagoon was indeed a community and everybody shared everything. One of the guys regularly took tourists out fishing. Most of the tourists only wanted to keep the trophy fish, or not the whole fish, so they just took what they wanted and we quite commonly had a community meal at the Poor Man's Bar with fresh fish right off the grill, and people would bring in their contributions, potatoes or other vegetables and fruits and whatever, and we had community meals. There were a number of children of all ages there, and during the daytime if a parent was working, there were always enough people to watch each other's kids. They spent the majority of their time on a smaller island called Happy Island, where their prime function was collecting hermit crabs. They'd hand out 5-gallon cans to collect the hermit crabs. At the end of the day, they would put them in screened cages and sell them, and the funds helped with birthday parties or whatever for the kids. So it was like a community center, where you could drop off the kids.

In the USVI, and later on Saint Maarten, I saw the importance of people working together to overcome all obstacles. One instance after hurricane Hugo struck the islands of St. Croix and St. Thomas pretty heavily, I was a part of a federal response team, FBI – HRT, that responded. When we landed, there were airplanes on their backs, mud everywhere, and trees down. Looking around, we quickly spotted two half-ton trucks and pickups that were marked as belonging to the USVI National Guard. However, looking into the vehicles and seeing the people moving around, I was amazed to see kids from age 14 on up on board. These were not national guardsmen; these were community members helping the national guardsmen. They would get out like ants and go into a house and salvage as much as they possibly could, into the back of the truck. They would bring it to higher ground and squeeze it into somebody else's house, if the roof could offer some protection.

There are other extenuating circumstances with hurricane Hugo, and that was due to the improper perception that was projected, but mainly spread by television, that the prison had been breached and that the island was covered with prisoners including robbers, etc. When we got there, we found that the prisons had been opened for a number of reasons. One, prisoners would not have survived if they stayed locked in their cells. Two, prison staff had their own families to worry about, and a large number of them had returned home to take care of their families. The one thing that in retrospect looking at it was, the overall impression I got, and the experiences I had were that these people were just trying to survive. The prisons in the USVI generally do not maintain death-row criminals, as those are sent to the federal penitentiaries in the Continental US. So, a lot of these people were in there for drugs or minor burglaries. It was not uncommon to see rows upon rows of shopping carts going down the street. Nothing like we see in our stateside riots. What happened was, here were people gathering stuff and paying what they felt was needed, and walking back to their communities to help their families out, and it was just unbelievable. When we got to handing out MREs, some people asked for extras for the lady down the street. When we gave it to them, they would walk down the street back to the door and see that the lady got her food and water. It was a totally different perception, that scene and other disaster situations, where selfish people take advantage for their own personal gain. It is a different way of life, and when people need help there is very little to no hesitation to help other people. There is good in all of us, and I saw that time and time again there in the USVI.

In addition to the National Guard and FBI troops in the area, the US Marines were there for Hurricane Hugo relief efforts. For those of you who are not aware, the USVI are right on the path of drug trafficking. One night, we were sitting in the hotel, we got a call to get to the shore quickly and went sneaking down there. We found US Marines with night-vision goggles waving us down. As we went closer to the shore, it looked like somebody had sprinkled popcorn in the ocean. The Marines had found glowsticks bobbing in the water, each one attached to a bale of cocaine. They had a couple of bales already, and we quickly started gathering the rest of the packages. One of the things consideration had to be given to, was how would this stuff be disposed of. When asked who would know that we had gathered this contraband, the decision was made that the bales had been dropped to be picked up by some bad guys, and that the bad guys were gonna have a difficult time explaining to their bosses where the stuff was. It was considered that the best thing to do was to just make it disappear with no word about it to anybody. Those bags disappeared and we never heard another thing about it, but I assumed there was a large, large volume of money lost over that. I would have loved to have heard the explanation from the guys who were supposed to pick that stuff up.

I was in the USVI for two or three hurricanes. On another occasion we found ourselves at an airport, and observed pallets of MREs and water. This was all stacked along the inner perimeter of the fence securing the airport. Outside the fence were many, many individuals looking for food but the government had not yet determined a distribution plan. After seeing how screwed up this was, I determined it was time to make a trip into some of the nearby communities, and as the back of the SUV was empty, we loaded it up with MREs and water. We drove out into a community, pulled into the middle of the street, opened the back door and handed supplies out to the people. We did this like four times until we were denied repeat access and they came up with a plan for distribution.

In the bad areas after these storms, rather than have their buildings torn apart, the majority of business owners (with the exception of jewelers) opened up the stores, stood there and told the people to go ahead and take the stuff, because they had insurance and it was better than having the building looted and burned to the ground.

Because I didn't want to cancel a scheduled EMT test, I had to ride out another storm – a hurricane in St. Maarten. I arrived on the last plane going in before it hit, but did have to cancel the test, and spent most of my time at a radio station in a concrete, cinder-block building. It was 2-1/2 stories high and it was right on the waterfront, so we had a hill washing down in front of us and also off to the left. To the right was a marine terminal, which was filled with containers from cargo ships. They ended up breaking loose and banging up against the building. There was no electricity in the building for the radio station or anything else, but they found an SUV that had an inverter, and drove it up on the side of the hill. We spliced extension cords together, plugged it in and brought it in and put it into the transmitter. That gave us power for the radio. We took out light bulbs inside to save energy, but kept on the outside lights. We sat in the dark and were able to radio out to a neighboring island, where they picked up the signal and transmitted it to Holland. I got to broadcast on the radio as Big Louie. It was also broadcast on the internet and before long we were getting calls reporting locations of flooding and damage, as well as people looking for friends and loved ones trying to reconnect.

Two of us sat in the radio station behind the mic for the following 2-1/2 or 3 days knowing that our calls were being picked up sporadically and sent on the Internet, and so we were not really out of touch. Eventually we sent people up to get more gasoline to keep the SUVs that were providing the electricity running. Eventually we felt pretty secure in the concrete building. That security was questioned a little bit when the empty containers started washing back-and-forth against the building. The wind and the howling were terrible, and it was totally dark in the building, so the only thing we could do was to have one of the windows with the hurricane shutters cocked open just a little so some light could come in. The owner of the building told us that the building was secure, that he had just had a new roof put on it. Unfortunately, shortly thereafter we started hearing a bit of banging, and we could look up at the ceiling and see daylight out through different sections. They had poured 2 inches of concrete over the existing roof, but they had not tied it to the side walls, so it was sitting there, laying on top of the building, not secured at all.

It was difficult to explain to some of the people that even though the rain stopped, they should stay in their homes or send one person to look for a place that was safer for them to go to.

By the time Hurricane Katrina hit the US in 2005, I was retired from the state and running my own business, Emergency Training Associates. But I was there in New Orleans for a conference, and lost thousands of dollars' worth of merchandise. My wife and I made it out on one of the last flights before the storm hit.

US HIGH DIVE TEAM

I n 1979, a newspaper article appeared stating that NBC's Sports World was going to have coverage of a world high-diving record breaking attempt from the Baltimore Inner Harbor, during the Baltimore City Fair. Interested in this, I found out where the US High Dive Team was practicing, and drove over to Cascade Lake to see them training. Meeting one of the divers, Doug Jones, I was amazed that anyone would attempt a high dive like that. I quickly realized that this was nothing new to this individual and his partners. I observed some practice, where they'd dive off and enter the water feet first. I learned you always landed feet first with your arms crossed tight across your chest. So, I watched a couple of dives, and we got to talking, and I asked him what the hell he was gonna do if somebody got hurt out there. And he says, "Bleed a lot, I guess." I learned more about their planned dive, and entry into the water, etc. The world record was 158 feet. Doug planned to dive from a 70-ton crane from as high as 180 feet. We estimated he'd hit the water at around 75 MPH.

There was much concern from both the city Police and Fire Departments over the danger of this dive, especially considering the unknown obstructions in the harbor that could include crumbling rebar and other debris, and not knowing how deep the water was, but the Fire Department did say that they would stand by. At a joint meeting, the Police Department stated that probably the best thing they could do, would be to climb the crane and arrest him for attempted suicide, considering the quality of the water. The other solution they mentioned was simply putting a net under the water so when he went in, they could pull the net up with his body. These were serious considerations.

Another paramedic training specialist, Ron Schaefer from MIEMSS, and I attended the event, and stationed ourselves in a rescue boat in the harbor. His entry was supposed to be feet-first, with arms folded across his chest. He actually entered the water more in a seated position. It wasn't a pretty dive, but as the only participant all he really had to do was survive. Upon entering the water, he quickly disappeared and we held our breath for him to come back up. When he surfaced, he had blood coming out of his nose and mouth, and we hollered for him to look at us, to make sure he was alert. No assistance or contact was allowed, or the dive would be disqualified and wouldn't break the record. We followed him with the boat, not touching him, and he swam to the dock and climbed up. A TV announcer interviewed him, and then we took him to our trailer, from where we took him to the Shock Trauma Unit, where it was determined he had broken both of his forearms. Luckily, he had no internal injuries. One of the precautions for high divers is to wear multiple canvas bathing suits, so they do not get 'atomic enemas.' As both of his arms were broken, I was awarded the opportunity to remove his bathing suits. I saw first-hand the toll a dive like that takes on a body.

Having survived this dive, the US High Dive Team went on to international competitions. I joined the team on the cliffs of Acapulco, Mexico from 1980 to 1984 as their Medical Safety Director. There were also Mexican, Italian, Canadian and British dive teams there.

After being in Acapulco a couple of times, the local kids recognized me as El Medico. Around 12-14 years old, they were there to greet us at the hotel. They stayed outside the doors at night, and in the morning, we would find fresh water at our door. I later found out it wasn't some good, fresh water; they just used the garden hose to fill the pots. But offering their assistance, they would scurry like mountain goats up and down the rocks, barefoot, to bring my medical equipment to the edge of the water, while I crawled white-knuckled to the edge. They seemed to admire my tennis shoes, so once before I left,

I gave one of the kids the pair I'd been using. Of course, they were too big and looked like clown shoes, but he was happy to get them. I was really moved when he didn't just throw his old ones away. He passed them on to someone else, so the gift kept giving.

It was a great time, except when one of the divers hit the rocks during practice. He tore up his leg and was hospitalized. They released him back to the hotel with open drainage, loose dressings (no cast or immobilization) and very little pain medication. I contacted Shock Trauma and told them that I believed we had gas gangrene, and received directions from them about how to take care of him.

Attempting to improve on the little care that the hospital had provided, I made a posterior splint using 2 sticks from flags, and a few boxes of casting plaster. We mixed it up and applied it in the hotel bathtub, clogging the drain. I was able to get Nubain from the local drugstore, to give him some pain relief.

Part of the plan was to get him back to the Shock Trauma Unit and the hyperbaric chamber. It was difficult to work through the bureaucracy of transporting him home. We had to get a certificate stating he could fly, and confirmation that he probably had gas gangrene. I met with two doctors, who had their hands out for money in exchange for what we needed.

At the airport, the airline insisted we pay for 2 tickets for him, since he had to rest his leg on another seat in front of him. Travelling in shorts and t-shirts, we landed in Philadelphia during a snow and ice event. The airline staff wouldn't assist us in moving him off the plane, so baggage handlers came on board and we put him backwards in a wheelchair to move him. Once we got inside, we attempted to rent a vehicle that would provide appropriate seating. A number of Philadelphia's cops declined to assist, saying if they touched him, the only place they'd take him was to the local hospital. Luckily, a lady at the rental car counter found a station wagon, and while waiting she asked if he needed anything. He asked for a cup of tea, and was given a cup of hot water and a tea bag. I reached into my shirt pocket and grabbed something to stir it with. Unfortunately, what I grabbed was NOT a pen but a thermometer! The end promptly blew off and leaked mercury into his tea. Both he and I wondered what the f--- else could go wrong.

Finally, we got loaded into the station wagon and headed to Baltimore, alerting them we were on our way. When we arrived, a doctor from the admitting area met us outside with a gurney and it was determined that it was, in fact, gas gangrene. He was scheduled for several sessions in the hyperbaric chamber over a couple of weeks. He lived in New Jersey, and had no insurance. But when he was discharged, he stayed at my house, and his family visited him there. My neighbors vouched that he had been living there, so he qualified for state assistance to cover the medical bills. My son handled daily dressing changes on his gaping, open wound. So, his leg was saved and he went back to New Jersey for continued care. The best part of this situation, is that he later recovered to the point that he was able to get a job with UPS driving a truck and making deliveries.

On a different trip with the dive team, one of the divers whose girlfriend was present, decided to propose to her. I was honored to marry them in the bar there in Acapulco, using my Universal Church of Life ministerial credentials.

The team did a fire dive at night. They'd put on a long-sleeved sweatshirt or two and then they'd have a hoodie on, and they'd take a towel and they'd pour gas on the towel to soak it. And then you could hang it and let a lot of it drip out of there, and they'd put it around their neck. They'd have a wire that ran down to a switch in their hand, where they pushed the button. The wire ran back up to a battery inside a little baggie with gunpowder in it. It only took enough gunpowder like from a bullet, all you needed was something to light, and when they were ready, and of course when they put the gas filled towel around their neck, the fumes got into the wet sweatshirts that they had on, and then they'd go up in the head of it, too. The tricky part was, while they were up there getting ready, they're seeing where the wind is coming from, because while they're standing there once they're lit off, they don't just light themselves and jump, they light off and usually wave around for the crowd. But you've got this fire around your neck, so you've gotta keep your face turned so the wind is coming to you and you're not burning your face up, and then they would dive off. That was interesting to see how they do it. Sometimes they wouldn't have the gunpowder so they'd take the old flashbulbs that used to go in the cameras, they had a plastic case around them, so you'd take and you'd have the wires on the two things. But you'd take and break the plastic, and the inside stuff looked like steel wool, it would just 'pffft' so that flash would set it off. That was much easier than the bullet gunpowder.

HOSTAGE RESCUE TEAM

The Hostage Rescue Team (HRT) is a unit of the FBI. They are trained to rescue American citizens and allies who are held hostage by hostile forces like terrorists or criminals, and the team is also part of the Critical Incident Response Group that was formed in 1994.

While I was working for MIEMSS, I got a call that the FBI wanted to meet with me for lunch. I told Dr. Cowley, and he told me to meet with them and give them whatever they wanted. They had formed the HRT and were training at Quantico. The agents at the gun range were interested in learning how to care for injuries from chemicals and tear gas, and eye injuries from shrapnel, etc. Dr. Cowley had told me to check out the names on the wall when I visited Quantico, which I did. Turned out, his great uncle was on that wall; the third agent killed in the line of duty for the FBI.

After providing that training, I was approached by one of the lead agents for another meeting to discuss training all the HRT agents as EMTs.

Not everybody knew HRT was being formed. We did an 80-hour training course at Quantico, VA. They took the National Registry Exam, but for security reasons, there were no photos, and no real names were used. They all used my home address. You can imagine all the junk mail that started arriving at my house, trying to sell magazine subscriptions and gear to the new EMTs. My mailman was gracious enough to collect it all in one box and deliver it once a month so I could get it to the agents.

This was back in the day when you could smoke just about anywhere. So, while teaching the EMT class, I used a round ashtray in the classroom. When I came back after a break, the ashtray was moved near the door. Next break, there's a NO SMOKING sign where the ashtray had been. I told the class I felt like a puppy dog being trained to go outside.

The team had built a shooting house made of tires at Quantico, VA for live fire exercises. We invited Dr. Cowley to see the exercises that were being done as part of the final approval/commissioning as part of the FBI. Dr. Cowley noticed one of the agents in camouflage move, and remarked, "He's a bush!"

The team's final certification exercise before being commissioned was held in 1983. It was code named Operation Equus Red, and was held at Kirtland Air Force Base in New Mexico. That's when HRT became an officially designated specialty team.

We also trained military people from similar units, like Green Berets, Navy Seals and numerous foreign teams that would come to the US to train, and we would go there to train as well.

Working with HRT required, of course, confidentiality. We referred to most comrades with weird or funny nicknames to protect their identities. At a Christmas party in Washington, DC, my wife enjoyed meeting people and putting faces with names like the Mad Bomber, etc.

Dr. Cowley had told me to do whatever needed doing for HRT/FBI, and the FBI didn't want other people involved for security reasons. There was an administrative director at MIEMSS that was constantly questioning me about my activities. However, Dr. Cowley told me I would only answer to him, and if anybody had any problems to send them to him. Needless to say, this created conflict between the administrator and me, as I took my direction from Dr. Cowley and the HRT commander. I had a team pager, and would be notified what number to call for directions when I was being called into service.

I was once in San Francisco at an EMS conference, and received instructions to go to the airport and get on a plane. My tickets were waiting, and I flew to Oakdale, LA where Cuban prisoners had rioted and taken over the prison. As Oakdale settled down, I was sent to Atlanta, where a gentleman in military duty uniform and a civilian dressed in a suit stopped me as I got off the plane, asking for me by name. They grabbed my bags and we went out to a helicopter, which took us to the Federal penitentiary, where yet another large riot had occurred. Four or five prisoners would come out at a time to talk with HRT negotiators. One guy had to take a leak. Just so happened the 4 o'clock shift was lined up outside, in full gear, waiting to go in. The HRT commander lined them up on both sides of the hallway, and told them to put on their mean faces; no touching, just mean faces. His goal was for this guy to walk by, see what we had waiting for them, and tell the others when he went back inside.

While I was there in Atlanta, I got a call from the head of the HRT in Washington, wanting me to identify the MIEMSS administrator who had been calling FBI offices to track me down. The FBI was concerned as to who this person was and what he wanted, as they understood I was operating under the direction of Dr. Cowley and no one else. I contacted the MIEMSS communication system (SYSCOM) and was informed that the communications director had been told to provide all the recordings from my calls to the administrator. Lo and behold, though, all of the tapes had been re-used or written over, and were unavailable.

When I returned home from Atlanta, I went directly to Dr. Cowley and explained to him the concerns of the FBI. He called in the administrator and his assistant, we all sat down and Dr. Cowley explained to the administrator that his actions were totally unacceptable, and reiterated that I worked for, and would report directly to, him, Dr. Cowley.

After that meeting, it became obvious that the administrator would take any and all steps to curtail my activities. I wasn't invited to as many meetings. However, my long-time friendship with and accessibility to Dr. Cowley only infuriated the administrator more. I had served many years as the National Registry State and Regional Coordinator, working closely with Rocco Morando, the Director of the National Registry. At a meeting in Philadelphia of the American Society of Testing Materials, in a crowded open hallway, the administrator announced to Mr. Morando that he was going to assign my assistant to take over my Registry duties. This announcement was made publicly in an attempt to curtail my activities. Mr. Morando responded that as the administrator of the state of Maryland, the administrator certainly could assign a replacement. He also stated that no matter who was assigned, that I would remain as the Regional representative, and the newly-named state representative would report to me. Rocco then turned to me and issued a 2-word closing statement, out in the open hallway as well: "F--- him!"

In 1976, Operation Liberty Sail was held in New York/New Jersey during the 4th of July Bi-Centennial. Tall ships from around the world were there. I was with HRT, staying in Ft. Monmouth, New Jersey providing security along with Navy, Coast Guard and NY Maritime Police. We flew around in two helicopters. Flying back, one guy yelled, "Look, a nude beach!" So, of course the pilots swung by and everybody strained to see, and all we saw was a gay, nude beach, and all the men were waving at us.

In April 1985 a standoff took Place with Covenant, Sword and Arm of the Lord in Mountain Home, Arkansas. 100+ state and Federal officials surrounded the group on a 240-acre compound with 14 buildings on 10 acres in the center of the property.

There was a kitten crawling around us while we were staked out in the woods. It got run over by a vehicle, and it's back half was mush. I guess since I was the medical advisor, I was elected to handle it. Being hidden in the woods, I couldn't shoot it to put it out of its misery, so I took it to the creek and put it in the creek under a rock. Afterward, our leader told everybody, "For Heaven's sake, if you get injured, don't call Lou!"

When I stopped working for the state in 1986, I continued as Field Services Advisor and Trainer for HRT, and went to Washington Hospital Center (MedStar) and hooked them up with HRT for medical services.

In 1987, I joined HRT in Indianapolis. A Cuban team was attending the Pan Am Games, and there was a perceived threat. HRT was there to intercede if it became necessary. Fortunately, it wasn't.

In 1988 an incident known as the Singer-Swapp Standoff, happened in Summit County, Utah. Correctional officer Lt. Fred House was shot and killed while he was trying to arrest brothers, who were suspected of aiding the bombing at Kamas State Center in Marion, Utah.

The Mormons were home-schooling kids and complained the local sheriff department was harassing them and were gonna take their kids. Singer went down to his mailbox, armed, and the cops killed him in a shootout. Three days later a court ruled the family could keep their kids and continue home schooling them.

They lived in close proximity to the Mormon house of worship. The house of worship was blown up, causing local law enforcement to call for assistance. Fresh snow was on the ground, and there were footprints from the home, to the house of worship, and back, giving a clue as to who had blown up the house of worship. Residents of the home which included children, were well-armed. It was considered a Federal case, and a stand-off started. I was on the team of Feds and local law enforcement, positioned in the remains of the house of worship. We stayed for days trying to negotiate for them to come out, but were unsuccessful.

Here and at the site of the Atlanta prison incident, satellites from Japan and other foreign countries were broadcasting, and the people inside could see what we were doing outside. A case of the media not being very helpful.

Twice at night, we moved into buildings that were closer to the home. At this point, there was only a field separating us, where goats grazed. Every morning, two people would come out with rifles over their shoulders, milk the goats, and take the milk back to the house. We played loud music to irritate them, to no avail.

So one morning two brothers came out to milk the goats. Then the front door opened and a K-9 dog came out, and the shooting started. A kid in a wheelchair in the doorway shot a cop. HRT couldn't fire back because there were kids in there. The older brother who was in the field got shot, and as the gunfire continued the commander and I ran to the back of the house. We used a ladder to climb into the house, and I was moving so fast that rather than using the steps, I used the crossbars on the back of the ladder, and someone had to reach out and pull me in the window by my arms.

Bullets were tearing through the house we were in, and vinyl, foam and wood pieces were flying everywhere. Spices were being blown out of the kitchen cabinets and scattered all over. I grabbed the injured officer and pulled him behind the refrigerator. One of the agents was being attacked by a dog, and he just fed the dog his arm, and while the dog stayed clamped on him, he dragged it upstairs and threw it in a room, closing the door. As they were going into the house, the commander took the guy who had been shot in the field.

An armored personnel carrier (like a tank without a cannon) was brought to the front of the house. We ripped down a closet door and I put the injured officer on it, then took him out to the armored personnel carrier, and from there into a helicopter. (I was later told that the armored personnel carrier took over 50 bullets.) There were heavy clouds, and we were in the mountains. We heard a voice on the radio from a military airport, telling us to keep our elevation up. Then a civilian voice told us to follow them, that they'd lead us in. A little twin-engine plane appeared on our side, and then went down through the clouds, and we followed. There was nothing I could do for the injured officer. Days later, the group finally surrendered.

I once went to Panama to bring back an injured American law enforcement officer who was traveling with the Secretary of State and had fallen on a large boat. I started at Andrews AFB, taking a full-body vacuum splint, and not much other equipment. I was dressed in civilian clothes, and went into the waiting area where 2 women in Air Force uniforms were behind a desk. I waved to them and sat down. Nobody said much to me at all, except a girl who came over to ask me if I was there to fix the heat. Then the phone rang, and somebody asked for me, so they started paying me some attention, at least offering me coffee. I followed an FBI pilot and a civilian contract pilot to a brand-new Lear jet (courtesy of a drug dealer who never got the chance to use it). It still had the plastic on the seats and tape on the drawers.

We took off, and landed in Mexico to fuel up. No flight plan had been filed, and the pilots walked into the building ahead of me. When I got there, they were getting grief about paperwork, insurance, etc. and were handing over money to the guy behind the counter. I went back out to the plane, and a guy from Immigration came over, holding a can of Lysol, saying he needed to fumigate the plane. I told him no, and showed him the medical supplies, trying to explain he couldn't fumigate the plane. Took some convincing, but after handing him $20, he sprayed a quick shot of Lysol into the air and went away.

Then we took off to Panama. It was cloudy and dark, and started lightning. The pilot turned the plane, trying to fly away from the lightning I guess; I couldn't see much out the side window. Then he says, "There it is." As we start to go down and come in, a voice comes over the radio, and tells us to land on the right side, because they were taking fire from the left side. When we landed, there were military jeeps with 50-caliber machine guns running on either side of us.

After we came to a stop and opened the door, a civilian vehicle came up and the pilots got off. I follow, and I hear, "Hey, Lou, what are you doing here?" It was a secret service agent I had trained as an EMT in Quantico. We got in a van, and he told me we were going to the naval base. There were road-blocks, Panamanian soldiers everywhere, and tires burning in the streets. We stopped and went into the front of a building, and walked right through, out the back door, and into another van. When we arrived at the naval base, we headed to the officers' mess, and the Panamanians asked to see our orders. We're starved, and now we're starting to get upset. A guy comes walking by on his way out of the mess, and says, "Hey, Lou, what are you doing here?" It was a Delta Force Doctor who I had been with at the Penitentiary in Atlanta with the HRT, during the riots in 1987. He showed the guards his orders and said we were under HIS orders. When we finally sat down to eat, the pilot asked, "Who the hell ARE you?" The following morning, I tended to the patient and brought him home.

In August 1991, I joined in on a rescue operation of 9 people who were taken hostage at the prison in Talladega, Alabama. Cuban inmates were trying to block their deportations back to Cuba, and had raised a Cuban flag over the prison. Once order was restored, 32 of them were deported.

I also participated with FBI/HRT during and after some tropical storms and hurricanes, which I talked about in the chapter titled *Islands*.

AMERICAN POWER BOAT ASSOCIATION

One morning around 1978, I was awakened by the sound of numerous chainsaws in my neighborhood. At this time, I was living in a house close by the water, and there had been talk about putting in sidewalks all the way down to the park. Here I was spending the morning not being able to sleep because of noise; but it didn't sound like construction noise. I went down to the park where I counted 45 boat trailers, and boats in the water racing back and forth. These were not chainsaws - these were really fast outboard motors. They were on boats the same style as a cigarette boat, only smaller, and only had one person inside. They were jumping out of the water and when they turned, it seemed like they stood straight up in the air.

The drivers were not restrained. They had no seatbelts or anything else for protection, but sat in the seat and with two hands on the steering wheel they held themselves in place. I inquired what happened if somebody got flipped out. I was pointed to one of the other boats sitting by the dock, and told, "We'll send him out and he'll just go grab the driver by the collar of his life jacket and pull him up on the deck." I turned around and, seeing my state vehicle all decorated with Shock Trauma and red lights, it was pretty difficult for me to accept that this was appropriate rescue care.

I talked to the people there, and they said that they would be happy to have us help. I was back off to talk to Dr. Cowley, and told him that I could make a shock trauma rescue unit on a boat. There were many different areas where we could supplement local EMS. He told me if I could get the boat and trailer, he would have no problem authorizing it as the designated Shock Trauma boat. I went to a couple of the drivers' meetings, and we purchased a boat and trailer with driver donations.

We held classes and worked with local dive rescue people and fire people, and met nice people at races that took place in our community and throughout Region 4.

The rescue boat became a family affair. We converted an old school bus to haul the boat and gear in, and upgraded to a bigger boat. We traveled the East Coast every weekend during the season, covering close to 20 races a year. My sons and daughter were crew members, and we did have to rescue quite a few friends. Later, we upgraded to a motorhome and two boats on a tandem trailer.

Our operation worked by integrating the local resources into the team, providing them the opportunity to participate and maintain a level of local control. We quickly learned that incorporating specialized local resources virtually eliminated negative contact and grew the team in size and capability. Over the years we covered races ranging from small boats that looked like backboards with alcohol powered outboards, to the Unlimited hydroplanes.

We traveled as a family almost every weekend from February through October and we expanded outside of Region 4, covering races from Valley Field, Canada to the Bahamas. Eventually my role morphed into the position of National Safety and Rescue Director for the American Power Boat Association.

We made great progress and received a lot of support from the racers. The exception being, the nemesis of, get ready for this... some of the dirtiest words I know... politics and lawyers.

As we developed a list of equipment we wanted on board, simple items such as a screwdriver, pliers or a prybar, lawyers stated "no". We could not add any tools to the medical equipment, because - get ready for this - what if we were going to a rescue and needed a pair of pliers to open a cockpit door or to cut a steering cable? Regardless of how helpful or necessary, if it wasn't officially approved, it wasn't allowed.

Earlier I mentioned Valleyfield, Canada. When we were there in 1996, the race was interrupted by a blimp crashing on the race course. We pulled two people out the window, and pushed the blimp to shore. They made repairs, and later took off again, and the races continued.

In 1998, I received the APBA Fred Hallet Memorial Leadership Award for 20 years of service as Medical Safety Director/Safety & Rescue Chairman. By the time I retired from APBA, Region 4's rescue team had grown into two boats, and added jet skis.

AFTERWORD

Over the years, Lou wrote many articles for the Maryland EMS Newsletter and other publications, and served as Associate Editor for both Firefighter News Magazine and EMS News Magazine, and as Assistant Editor for Rescue News. For a time, he was also involved in publishing.

In 1979, he started Emergency Training Associates, out of his home. That company grew into a large family business, with 15 employees providing training services and materials, gear, gifts and apparel for the fire, EMS, police and medical communities until 2016.

In addition to lots of travel to trade shows and conferences, he participated in and supported several initiatives, including Police Week in DC, memorial rides and others. At the annual National Fallen Firefighters memorial ceremonies, he was honored to present each family with a bumper sticker bearing the name of their loved one.

He supported his local Fire Company, Union Bridge Fire Company in Maryland since 1995, serving as Public Information Officer and Carroll County Fire Police Officer.

After moving the family business to a larger space in Carroll County, Maryland, ETA joined the Taneytown Chamber of Commerce and, in 2007/2008, Lou served as President of the Chamber. He was awarded the President's Award for Outstanding Leadership in 2012.

He was also active with the Taneytown Lion's Club, and one of his favorite activities was playing Santa for the town's children.

Lou also enjoyed driving the trolley for Lorien Health Care residents in Taneytown. He seemed happiest, though, when his family was gathered together.

TIMELINE/HIGHLIGHTS IN MARYLAND AND NATIONAL EMS

1969

Center for the Study of Trauma (now Shock Trauma Center) was completed and officially opened.

US DOT funding was obtained for the first civilian air med-evac program in the US. Dr. Cowley and MD state police developed program of evacuating accident victims by helicopter. First time was in March 1970 on I-695 at Falls Road, victim taken to Shock Trauma Unit. Used roof of adjacent garage as heliport.

Hyperbaric Medicine Center was designated a specialty referral center.

1970

Efforts begun to educate ambulance personnel, establish standards of emergency care and develop transportation and communications systems.

1972

84-hour EMT-Ambulance (EMT-A) program BLS and 140-hour CRT program developed and implemented.

1973

Governor Mandell created the Division of EMS (DEMS) in the Dept of Health & Mental Hygiene, and also MIEM in University of MD (formerly the Center for the Study of Trauma).

1974

EMS Newsletter started under Division of MD Dept of Health & Mental Hygiene. Five regions: Appalachian Region (Alleghany and Garrett Counties); Mid-MD (Frederick and Washington); Metro Baltimore (Baltimore City, Baltimore, Anne Arundel, Harford, Howard and Carroll); Eastern Shore (Cecil, Kent, Queen Anne's, Caroline, Talbot, Dorchester, Somerset, Wicomico and Worcester); and Metro Washington Region (Montgomery, Prince George's, Charles, Calvert and St. Mary's, 4 counties in DC and 2 cities in Northern Virginia). These regions comprised Regional Emergency Medical Services Advisory Council (REMSAC), which met quarterly.

Esophogeal airways were only allowed to be used by CRTs, and only if a doctor took responsibility for certifying the CRT was proficient in its use, and the physician assumed responsibility.

CRT courses piloted and begun at Sinai Hospital and Baltimore City Hospital and University of MD.

Baltimore City received first DOT grant in MD, one quarter million dollars to upgrade and improve ambulances and telecommunications and to initiate a telemetry system. Chief McMahon wrote the grant proposal.

1975

Existing specialty referral centers in Baltimore City became part of the MD EMS system.

First statewide EMS continuing education program for nurses established.

Maryland Fire & Rescue Institute began to assume responsibility of training EMT-A instructors and offering the majority of instructional programs for EMT-As.

Emergency Medical Communication System first total system to be implemented in MD. Emergency Medical Resources Center (EMRC) based at Sinai Hospital. SYSCOM, state-operated facility at MIEMSS, coordinated all med-evac transports by MD State Police, US Park Police, US Army and US Coast Guard.

1976

DEMS/MIEM hosted the first International EMS/Trauma Symposium in Baltimore. In conjunction, the first harbor disaster exercise.

First Annual EMS Olympics.

Beltsville man became first organ donor under 1974 law that permitted people to indicate they were an organ donor on a driver's license.

Good Samaritan law was signed.

Work begun to initiate a CPR program in secondary schools, in cooperation with the MD affiliate of the AHA.

1977

DEMS & MIEM combined into MIEMSS.

40-hour first responder course became part of the MIEMS training program for prehospital care providers.

1978

Mock Disaster held at BWI Airport, utilizing ambos from surrounding areas, MD state police helicopters and Army med-evac helicopters, demo of satellite transmission with NASA's Goddard Space Flight Center, Communications Satellite Labs (COMSTAT) and Office of Telecommunications of the MD State Center for Public Broadcasting. ATS-6 satellite, 22,000 miles above Christmas Island in the Pacific. O'Hare and Logan airports, CTS satellite to Brooke Army Medical Center in San Antonio. CTS also to VA hospital in Albuquerque NM.

First statewide EMS telecommunications system in the country was completed. Featured ECG telemetry and linked together specialty referral centers, hospital ERs, a fleet of MD State Police Med-Evac helicopters, and hundreds of ambulance companies.

Article on USVI. Star of Life II – at the time world's largest sea ambulance, at St. John.

Lou and others trained security officers for MD Thoroughbred Racing

Protective Bureau Association, in CPR, dedicated phone line put into Sinai for emergencies at Pimlico Racetrack in Baltimore, MD.

At Ocean City, MD Firefighter's Week, Lou demonstrated modified rope-sling rescue.

Ron Schaefer (Associate Director of Prehospital Education and Training) and Lou (Associate Director of Prehospital Care) conducted feasibility test by training 58 merchant ship officers who were attending the MEBA Engineering School. Found if officers on merchant ships had ALS training of 30 hours, significant numbers of heart attack victims could be saved.

1979

MIEMSS developed the 'Emergency Medical Guide' for the Baltimore Metro Yellow Pages in cooperation with C&P Telephone and Congresswoman Barbara Mikulski.

First group of medical students in MD required to take EMT course. Ron and Lou taught at Hopkins Medical School.

MIEMSS began 4-hour training program for prehospital care providers in the use of and application of the esophageal obturator airway and MAST garments.

1980

First MD EMS Week proclaimed by the Governor.

First course in emergency health sciences program was offered by MIEMSS in collaboration with UMBC.

Ad Hoc Committee on Training, Testing and Certification (consisting of representatives from MIEMSS, the MD State Firemen's Association, the MD State Ambulance and Rescue Association, the MD Council of Training Academies, the MD Fire and Rescue Institute and the MD Fire and Rescue Education and Training Commission) approved revision for the testing procedures used for the EMT practical exam. Students had complained that the skills procedures used for the practical were not stressed during the classroom instruction sessions or that equipment used during the practical was not the same as that used in the classroom, contributing to a high failure rate. Decided they could be immediately retrained and retested on one or two stations.

1981

EMT testing and certification decentralized from MIEMSS to regions.

MD State Police med-evac observers completed advanced training in trauma management to become the first aviation trauma technicians (ATTs).

1982

Draft of 'The MD Way' distributed.

Machine-read ambulance runsheets were first used in MD.

MIEMSS assumed an active role in developing a civilian/military contingency hospital system in Baltimore. Initiated by DOD to assess the personnel and physical capabilities of local hospitals in the event of an overseas conflict involving the US.

Planned for 1987

Increase Shock Trauma Center from 90,000 sf to 200,000 sf. 65 more beds, totaling 138. Three 12-bed critical care recovery units, three 12-bed intensive care units, and two 33-bed intermediate care units, one of which will include a 9-bed transitional rehab unit.

1983

Tom Baker testing Grand Prix racer Orange Crush, over 130 mph on Wye River. Friday the 13th, also the first day the MIEMSS/APBA rescue boat became operational. Used specially-designed hoist with stokes basket. Minor injuries, released within a few days. Registered as the Star of Life VI in the Star of Life Flotilla. Designed to provide immediate care and was staffed with fully trained volunteers. Doctors at MIEMSS Shock Trauma Center donated the first several hundred dollars to spark interest, and boat-racing drivers and fans accepted the challenge. Used marine radio to contact SYSCOM. Trained crew supplemented existing EMS providers.

MIEMSS established the National Study Center for Trauma and Emergency Medical Systems.

Ron and Lou attended 7th annual meeting of NCSEMSTC in Bismark, ND.

National study group established under a DOT grant to evaluate EMT matters (texts/lesson plans/audiovisuals/instructor training). Appointed co-chairs of the National Reciprocity Committee.

US DOT training program for EMT-paramedics recognized by MD General Assembly.

Agreement signed that MD, PA, VA, WV, DE, NJ and DC EMTs and CRTs could cross state lines to render care on an emergency, mutual-aid basis.

1984

EMT-A task force recommendations.

'The MD Way – EMT-A Skills Manual' published.

1985

Disaster exercise testing National Disaster Medical System (NDMS) and the MD Disaster Plan. 600 casualties were received at Andrews Air Force Base and BWI Airport, and transported to participating hospitals.

8th national trauma symposium sponsored by MIEMSS.

EMRC and SYSCOMM plan to merge, more base stations and new equipment for prehospital care providers.

Task force recommended to enhance the 84-hour EMT-A program to the national 110-hour program.

Two additional levels of advanced life support, ATT and EMT-P, recognized by Board of Medical Examiners in MD.

Paramedic examinations for national certification held in January 1985. By end of September, there were 124 in MD.

State-wide 911 emergency system of communication implemented on July 1.

New medical protocols for MD CRTs and EMT-Ps implemented.

Patient number 20,000 admitted to Shock Trauma Center in December.

1986

MD State Police Med-Evac crashed in Leakin Park. Was returning to Frederick barracks after transporting a shooting victim from Eldersburg to the MIEMSS Shock Trauma Center. Cpl. Gregory May and Tfc. Carey Poetzman, who was the first woman to join the aviation division of the MD State Police, both perished. Carey was an LPN and respiratory technician, an aviation trauma technician, and a medical specialist with the US Army Reserve.

Recent study showed accident victims in MD have a better chance of reaching a hospital alive than victims in the US as a whole. In1980 US=15% DOA, MD=6% DOA. In 1981 US=14.5% DOA, MD=5.6% DOA.

MIEMSS actively supported the successful legislation for a mandatory seatbelt law.

During NDMS-86, 1,000 casualties handled from mock disaster at the Capital Center. Happened in Novak Field House on the campus of PG Community College in Largo. Chinook and Huey helicopters, buses, army ambos and local ambos. Specially configured Amtrak train.

Big EMT-A program changes – New 110-hour MD EMT-A training and certification program approved for statewide implementation starting July 1. Integrated first-responder training with EMT-A training; the first 40 hours of the EMT course satisfied the first-responder requirements. This enabled the first responder to proceed to a higher level of training without the need for repetitive training. In effect, this modularized BLS training in the same manner in which ALS training was modularized.

MD, DC, VA EMS responded to a mock earthquake in Missouri as part of a drill by NDMS. 600 'victims' flown to BWI and Andrews AFB. Coordinated by MIEMSS.

EMT-D pilot program in MD to allow ALS providers to use an automatic defibrillator. Held in Calvert and Prince George's counties.

DC-MD Memorandum of Understanding between Dr. Cowley, Harry Hughes and Marion Barry. Provided guidelines when emergencies occur close to jurisdictional boundaries.

State-wide helicopter regulations for the first time to enhance safety and improve communications between helicopters and hospitals.

1987

Amtrak train with 650 persons from Newport News, VA to Boston, MA collided with a Conrail multi-engine train in Chase, MD. Disaster plan and 20-hospital alert issued. Requested 4 go-teams. Trauma Go-Teams consisted of a MIEMSS shock trauma surgeon or physician and a nurse from the admitting area. They carried their own supplies such as blood, blood products, and surgical and resuscitative equipment, and were prepared to perform stabilizing and resuscitative measures even during the course of extrication. Directed by the on-scene medical commander. 16 fatalities, 175+ treated at area hospitals, 400+ evaluated and processed through secondary triage and treatment center in Chase fire station.

25th anniversary of Shock Trauma Center.

$31 million fund established to replace MSP fleet with new twin-engine aircraft.

MIEMSS Task Force on AIDS established, whole newsletter devoted to AIDS. 'AIDS: A Guide for EMS' compiled and distributed.

1988

Governor Schaefer approved funding for equipping the new R Adams Cowley Shock Trauma Center, replacing and upgrading EMS Communications system, and enhancing training for pre-hospital care providers.

Shock Trauma Gala held, celebrating 15th anniversary of the MD EMS System.

New communications system established direct contact from SYSCOM to every MSP med-evac helicopter around the state.

Legislation passed requiring that first responders be notified if they have transported or treated someone with AIDS.

1989

$44 million new building at Penn and Lombard streets.

SYSCOM and EMRC merged, now in Dunning Hall adjacent to Shock Trauma Center.

First Dauphin helicopter operational. Specially designed state-of-the-art medical interior.

New heliport-the days of the dumpster are over (7 corkscrew levels down, down the street, offloaded near the dumpster).

Search Committee established for MIEMSS Director.

1990

Dr. James Flynn named Director of MIEMSS. Acting since 1989 when Cowley left to become director of the Charles McC. Mathias Jr. National Study Center for Trauma and EMS.